THE POCKET GUIDE TO
LGV DRIVERS' HOURS & TACHOGRAPH LAW

2nd edition

DAVID LOWE

**The Chartered Institute of
Logistics and Transport (UK)**

**KOGAN
PAGE**

Publisher's note

Every possible effort has been made to ensure that the
information contained in this book is accurate at the
time of going to press, and the publishers and author
cannot accept responsibility for any errors or omissions,
however caused. No responsibility for loss or damage
occasioned to any person acting, or refraining from
action, as a result of the material in this publication can
be accepted by the editor, the publisher or the author.

First published in Great Britain in 2002
Second edition 2004

Kogan Page Limited
120 Pentonville Road
London N1 9JN
United Kingdom
www.kogan-page.co.uk

British Library Cataloguing in Publication Data

A CIP record for this book is available from the British
Library.

ISBN 0 7494 4335 9

Typeset by Saxon Graphics Ltd, Derby
Printed and bound in Great Britain by
Bell & Bain, Glasgow

THE POCKET GUIDE TO
LGV DRIVERS' HOURS & TACHOGRAPH LAW

CONTENTS

PREFACE

This book combines information on drivers' hours with a guide to dealing with tachographs, as the topics covered are so relevant to each other. In addition, there is useful information on a number of related measures that affect large goods vehicle (LGV) drivers, namely:

- the working time regulations for road transport workers;
- the national minimum wage rules;
- the fitment and use of digital tachographs; and
- drugs, tiredness and stress.

The question might be asked as to why is it necessary to produce a book such as this, since the current European Union (EU) rules on driving times, breaks and rest periods for truck drivers, the British domestic rules and the record-keeping and tachograph rules have all been in existence, and largely unchanged, since 1986. However, despite this long passage of time, the fact is that these rules remain, for many drivers and operators in the road transport industry, a complex hotchpotch of legal mumbo-jumbo. The extensive reports in the weekly transport press, of prosecutions and of the severe penalties imposed on convicted offenders, is testimony to that confusion.

Tachograph offences are the number one LGV crime in England and Wales, with 5,694 convictions in 2002/03, closely followed by hours law offences for which 4,060 convictions were recorded in the same period. While it has to be recognized that some of the offences reported are quite deliberately committed for gain, the vast majority are the result of the unwitting action of drivers and operators who just do not know what the law requires of them. But deliberate or accidental, the fact remains that one of the surest ways of losing an LGV driving licence or an 'O' licence is to offend against the drivers hours and tachograph rules.

Besides the problems of compliance with the drivers' hours law and tachograph requirements, truck drivers are now having to come to terms with other key work-related issues such as the working time rules, minimum pay issues, and health matters such as drug abuse, tiredness and stress.

The purpose of this *Guide* is to explain all these issues in lay person's terms and to describe precisely what the law requires in order to help readers to avoid loss of their licences. It identifies which rules apply to which drivers; what exemptions apply and who is covered by them; what records must be kept and how this should be done; what effect the working time regulations have on the transport industry; and the minimum wage rules.

Altogether, this *Guide* provides drivers and truck operators with everything they need to know about compliance with the law on these difficult matters. By following the guidance given, they should avoid the risk of prosecution and save themselves a great deal of the money, heartache and hassle that inevitably follows such punitive action.

ABOUT THE AUTHOR

David Lowe has over 50 years' experience in the road haulage industry, much of it at a practical level both behind the wheel and as a hands-on fleet manager. Now widely known and respected as a freelance writer on transport law matters, he is the author of the *Transport Manager's and Operator's Handbook* which explains complex legal issues in readily comprehensible language, and many other transport study manuals and law guides. He has also written extensively on legal matters for the transport press.

EU AND AETR DRIVERS' HOURS

INTRODUCTION

European law requires that any person who drives a goods vehicle for commercial or business purposes must conform to strict rules on:

- the amount of time they may spend driving between breaks, in a day, in a week and in a fortnight;
- the minimum breaks to be taken during the driving day; and
- both minimum daily and weekly rest periods.

These rules do not apply where the vehicle:

- is being used for purely private purposes; or
- is specifically exempted from the rules as specified in the Appendix.

Breach of these rules, which are imposed in the interests of public safety, will lead to prosecution and severe penalty on conviction, as described later. Additionally, such convictions can have a serious impact on a driver's vocational driving entitlement (eg suspension or revocation of the driver's LGV driving licence) and result in the loss of his or her employer's 'O' licence.

Which rules apply?

Both vehicle operators and their drivers have a statutory duty to make sure that they clearly understand which set of rules applies, depending on the vehicle being driven or the nature of the transport operation on which they are engaged, and the specific requirements of those rules.

Three sets of rules apply as follows:

- the EU rules;
- the AETR rules for international journeys outside the EU (now fully aligned with the EU rules); and
- the British domestic rules.

The specific requirements of the EU and AETR rules are explained in this chapter. This will show which drivers must follow the rules and those that are exempt. The British domestic rules for drivers exempt from the EU rules are described fully in Chapter 4.

THE EUROPEAN UNION RULES

The current EU rules, contained in Regulation 3820/85/EC, came into effect in the UK on 29 September 1986. British regulations implementing these rules and modifying previous provisions came into effect on the same date and are listed below:

- The Community Drivers' Hours and Recording Equipment Regulations 1986 –

which made consequential changes to the 1968 Transport Act provisions.

- The Community Drivers' Hours and Recording Equipment (Exemptions and Supplementary Provisions) Regulations 1986 (as amended 1986, 1987 and 1988) – which implemented the EU regulations in the UK and the derogations (ie exemptions) from them.
- The Drivers' Hours (Goods Vehicles) (Modifications) Order 1986 – which implemented changes to national and domestic driving under the 1986 Act.
- The Drivers' Hours (Harmonization with Community Rules) Regulations 1986 – which harmonized the rules for those who drive under both the EU regulations and the revised 1968 Act rules.
- The Drivers' Hours (Goods Vehicles)(Exemptions) Regulations 1986.

NB: *Consideration is being given in Brussels to proposed changes to Regulation 3820/85/EC. These are itemized on pages 19–21.*

Vehicles covered

EU rules always take precedence over national rules. Therefore, since all goods vehicles and other vehicles used for the carriage of goods used in connection with business activities are covered by one or other of the sets of drivers' hours rules listed above (ie EU, AETR or British), the specific requirements of the EU rules must be considered first.

The first step involves examining the list of EU rules exemptions (called derogations in legal terminology) given in the Appendix to see whether the vehicle itself or the transport operation on which it is being used is shown.

This will identify whether an exemption applies, in which case the reader must then refer to the British domestic rules described in Chapter 4. If no exemption is shown, the EU rules described in this chapter must be followed.

It is important to note that for an exemption to apply, the terms in which it is described in the list must match exactly the vehicle or the operation in question. There is no legal margin for a vehicle or a use that is only somewhat similar to that described to be able to take advantage of the exemption.

To reiterate two key points regarding the exemptions list:

- where a vehicle has a permissible maximum weight (pmw) not exceeding 3.5 tonnes, it is exempt from the EU rules; or
- if the vehicle is one that is identified on the EU exemptions list or is used for a purpose which is shown in the list as exempt as mentioned previously (eg vehicles used by the public utilities and local authorities etc), it is automatically exempt.

In either case the vehicle automatically comes within the scope of the British domestic rules set out in the 1968 Transport Act as described in detail in Chapter 4.

Conversely, where vehicles are over 3.5 tonnes permissible maximum weight, including the weight of any trailer drawn, and are not shown on the exemptions list or are not used for an exempt purpose, the EU hours law as described in this chapter applies in full.

Off-road vehicles

The EU law also applies (since August 1998) to vehicles commonly described as 'off roaders' or '4 × 4s' that are being used for the carriage of goods and which, when towing trailers, have a combined weight (ie of the towing vehicle and the trailer) exceeding 3.5 tonnes.

Definitions

To apply the rules as required and appreciate their implications, it is necessary to understand the definitions of certain words and phrases used as follows.

Driver

The rules apply specifically to the 'driver' of the vehicle. This is any person who drives the vehicle, even for a short period, or who is carried on the vehicle ready to drive if necessary. They do not apply to persons carried as mates (ie to help load and unload only) or to statutory attendants carried on abnormal load operations.

Driving

Driving is time spent behind the wheel actually driving the vehicle. It does not include any other activities such as checking the vehicle or load, which counts as 'other work'.

Driving time

Driving time is the accumulation of periods spent driving:

- before a break must be taken or a daily rest period is started; or
- between two daily rest periods; or
- between a daily rest period and a weekly rest period.

Vehicle categories

Drivers of all types and weight categories of vehicles within the scope of the regulations are treated equally in regard to driving, break and rest periods.

A day

A day is any period of 24 hours starting from the time when a driver commences work after a daily or weekly rest period (ie when the tachograph is set in motion).

NB: If a vehicle to which the EU regulations apply is driven on any day (no matter how short the actual time spent driving or how short the journey on the road – even just 5 or 10 minutes down the road) then the legal requirements apply to the driver for the whole of that day (ie the 24-hour period) and the week in which that day falls.

Fixed week

A 'week' in the rules is a fixed week from 00.00 hours on Monday to 24.00 hours on the following Sunday.

NB: All references in the rules to weeks and weekly limits must be considered against this fixed week. Reference to 'fortnight' means two consecutive fixed weeks.

Working time (spread-over)

Time spent by a driver doing work other than driving must be recorded on the tachograph chart and counted along with driving in the 24-hour day. Thus, for example, drivers could drive for the normal daily maximum of 9 hours and take their 11-hour daily rest, leaving a further four hours in which they could work for their employer. At least 45 minutes of this time would need to be the statutory break they take during the driving day.

Under a recent ruling of the European Court of Justice, drivers who travel from their home to collect their vehicle from a place other than their employer's premises (ie operating centre) must now record that time as working time on the tachograph chart. Additionally, where tipping vehicles are driven on off-road sites, if the driver subsequently intends driving either that vehicle or another vehicle under the regulations (ie on the public highway), the time spent driving off-road must be counted as working time and recorded on the tachograph chart accordingly.

Employers' responsibilities

Employers must make sure that their drivers understand fully how the law applies to them and how to comply with its detailed provisions. They have specific responsibilities under the EU rules as follows:

- They must organize drivers' work in such a way that the rules are not broken (ie on driving times, breaks and rest periods etc).
- They must make regular checks – of tachograph charts, for example – to ensure the law is complied with.
- Where they find any breaches of the law by drivers, they must take appropriate steps to prevent any repetition of such offences.

NB: Although it is no excuse in court for a driver to say that he or she did not know the law, the court would expect the employer to have instructed the driver in its requirements and may well convict the employer for 'failing to cause' the driver to conform to the law (or for permitting offences) if it felt that insufficient attention had been given to this matter.

Driving limits

Goods vehicle drivers are restricted in the amount of time they can spend driving:

- before taking a break;
- between any two daily rest periods (or a daily and a weekly rest period);
- in a week; and
- in a fortnight.

Calculation of the driving period begins at the moment when the driver sets his or her tachograph in motion and begins driving. The maximum limits are as follows:

- Maximum driving before a break: 4½ hours
- Maximum daily driving normally: 9 hours
- Extended driving on 2 days
  in week only: 10 hours
- Maximum weekly driving: 6 daily
                                     driving shifts*
- Maximum fortnightly driving
  (ie in 2 consecutive weeks):   90 hours

*NB: The High Court ruled in 1988 that drivers can exceed the maximum of six daily driving shifts within six days as specified in the EU rules provided they do not exceed the maximum number of hours permitted in six consecutive driving periods.

Where a driver spends the maximum amount of time driving in one week (ie 4 × 9 hours plus 2 × 10 hours = 56 hours), during the next following fixed week he or she may drive only for a maximum of 34 hours to conform to the 90-hour two-weekly maximum.

Break periods

Drivers are required by law to take a break or a number of breaks if in a day the aggregate (ie total amount) of their driving amounts to 4½ hours or more. If they do not drive for 4½ hours in the day there is no legal requirement for them to take a break during that day.

Break periods must not be counted as part of a daily rest period, and during breaks the driver must not do any 'other work'. However, 'other work' does not include:

- waiting time;
- time spent riding as a passenger in a vehicle; or
- time spent on a ferry or train.

The requirement for taking a break is that, immediately the 4½-hour driving limit is reached, a break of 45 minutes must be taken, unless a daily or weekly rest period starts at that time. This break may be replaced by a number of other breaks of *at least* 15 minutes each spread over the driving period, or taken during and immediately after this period, so as to equal at least 45 minutes and taken in such a way that the 4½-hour maximum driving limit is not exceeded.

According to the European Court, where a 45-minute break has been taken either as a single break or as several breaks of at least 15 minutes each during or at the end of a 4½-hour driving period, the calculation of driving times begins afresh, without taking into account the driving time and breaks previously completed.

It is important to note that a break period which *was* due does not have to be taken if, immediately following the driving period, the driver starts a daily or weekly rest period, so long as the 4½ hours maximum driving is not exceeded.

DfT examples show that the driver could legally operate the following procedures:

- Drive 1 hour, 15 minutes' break, drive 3½ hours, 30 minutes' break, drive 1 hour, 15 minutes' break, drive 3½ hours, commence daily rest period.
- Drive 1 hour, 15 minutes' break, drive 1 hour, 15 minutes' break, drive 2½ hours, 15 minutes' break, drive 2 hours, 30 minutes' break, drive 2½ hours, commence daily rest period.
- Drive 3 hours, 15 minutes' break, drive 1½ hours, 30 minutes' break, drive 3 hours, 15 minutes' break, drive 1½ hours, commence daily rest period.

Any break taken in excess of the required 45 minutes after driving for 4½ hours cannot be counted as part of the break period legally required in respect of the next 4½-hour driving period.

NB: It is important to note that break periods (ie especially the 45-minute period as well as the alternative minimum 15-minute periods) should not be curtailed even by a minute or two. Prosecutions have been brought for offences relating to break periods that are alleged not to conform to the law even though they have been only a matter of minutes below the minimum specified in the rules. These timings are, of course, shown clearly on tachograph recordings which provide ample evidence for the prosecution case.

Rest periods

Rest periods are defined as uninterrupted periods of at least one hour during which the driver 'may freely dispose of his time'. Daily rest periods, and particularly rest periods which are compensating for previously reduced rest periods, should not be confused with, or combined with, statutory break periods required to be taken during the driving day as described above.

It has been held that time spent by drivers on weekend training courses (eg Hazchem courses and such like), even where there is no direct payment of wages by the employer, breaches the requirements under EU rules for drivers to have a period of weekly rest during which they may freely dispose of their time.

Daily rest

Once each day, drivers are required to take either a normal, a reduced or a split daily rest period during which time they must be free to dispose of their time as they wish. These daily rests are to be taken once in each 24 hours starting when the driver activates the tachograph following a daily or weekly rest period.

Where the daily rest is taken in two or three separate periods (see below), the calculation must commence at the end of a rest period of not less than eight hours. Thus in each 24-hour period one or other of the following daily rest periods must be taken:

- Normal daily rest:
  11 hours

or alternatively:

- Reduced rest (max 3 times weekly):
  9 hours – the reduced time must be compensated by an equal amount of additional rest taken with other rest periods

before the end of the next following fixed
week.
- Split rest:
  Where the daily rest period is not reduced
  (as above) the rest may be split and taken
  in two or three separate periods during the
  24 hours, provided:
  - one continuous period is of at least 8
    hours' duration;
  - other periods are of at least 1 hour's
    duration;
  - the total daily rest period is increased to
    12 hours.

Split daily rest
When a daily rest period is split into two or
three separate periods, the eight-hour period
must be in the last portion of the rest (under a
European Court ruling).

Double-manned vehicles
Where a two-person crew operates a vehicle,
the daily rest period requirement is that each
person must have had a minimum of 8 hours'
rest in each period of 30 hours. Daily rest,
however, cannot be taken on a moving vehicle
(see below).

   A double-manned vehicle can be driven
for a maximum of 20 hours within the 22-hour
period left after deducting eight hours' rest from
the 30-hour spread-over mentioned above –
each crewmember driving for 10 hours.

NB: It should be noted that the law applies to
both crewmembers from the commencement of
the journey (or their day's work if that
commenced earlier).

Daily rest on vehicles

Daily rest periods may be taken on a vehicle provided:

- the vehicle has a bunk so the driver (but not necessarily a mate or attendant) can lie down; and
- the vehicle is stationary for the whole of the rest period.

It follows from this that a driver on a double-manned vehicle cannot be taking part of his or her *daily rest period* on the bunk while the co-driver continues to drive the vehicle. The driver could, however, be taking a *break* at this time while the vehicle is moving, or could merely spend the time lying on the bunk with his or her tachograph chart recording 'other work'.

Daily rest on ferries/trains

Daily rest periods which are taken when a vehicle is to be carried for part of its journey on a ferry crossing or by rail may be interrupted *once only* provided that:

- part of the rest is taken on land before or after the ferry crossing/rail journey;
- the interruption is 'as short as possible' and in any event not more than one hour before embarkation or after disembarkation and includes dealing with customs formalities;
- during both parts of the rest (ie in the terminal and on board the ferry/train) the driver has access to a bunk or couchette;
- when such interruptions to daily rest occur, the total daily rest period is extended by two hours.

Weekly rest

Once each fixed week (and after six driving shifts – see note on page 8), a daily rest period must be combined with a weekly rest period to provide a weekly rest period totalling 45 hours. A weekly rest period that begins in one fixed week and continues into the following week may be attached to either of these weeks.

While the normal weekly rest period is 45 hours as described above, this may be reduced to:

- 36 hours when the rest is taken at the place where the vehicle or driver is based; or
- 24 hours when the rest is taken elsewhere.

Reduced weekly rest periods must be compensated (ie made up) by an equivalent amount of rest period time taken:

- *en bloc*;
- added to another rest period of at least 8 hours' duration; and
- before the end of the third week following the week in which the reduced weekly rest period was taken.

Compensated rest periods

When reduced daily and/or weekly rest periods are taken, the compensated time must be:

- attached to another rest period of at least eight hours' duration; and
- granted, at the request of the driver, at the vehicle parking place or at the driver's base.

Compensation in this respect *does not* mean compensation by means of payment; it means the provision of an equivalent amount of rest time taken on a later occasion but within the specified limits, ie:

- by the end of the next week for compensated daily rest; and
- by the end of the third following week in the case of compensated weekly rest period; and
- in either case added to other rest periods.

Summary of EU rules

The following table summarizes the EU rules applicable to both national and international goods vehicle operations as described above:

- Maximum daily driving:
  9 hours
  10 hours on 2 days in week.
- Maximum weekly driving:
  6 daily driving periods.
- Maximum fortnightly driving:
  90 hours.
- Maximum driving before a break:
  4½ hours.
- Minimum breaks after driving:
  45 minutes or other breaks of at least
  15 minutes each to equal 45 minutes.
- Minimum daily rest (normally):
  11 hours.
- Reduced daily rest:
  9 hours on up to 3 days per week (must be made up by end of next following week).
- Split daily rest:
  The 11-hour daily rest period may be split into two or three periods – one at least
  8 hours, the others at least 1 hour each:
  total rest must be increased to 12 hours.
- Minimum weekly rest (normally):
  45 hours once each fixed week.

- Reduced weekly rest:
  36 hours at base – 24 hours elsewhere
  (any reduction must be made up *en bloc* by
  end of the third following week).
- Rest on ferries/trains:
  Daily rest may be interrupted once only if:
  - part taken on land;
  - no more than 1 hour between parts;
  - drivers must have access to a bunk or
    couchette for both parts of rest;
  - total rest must increase by 2 hours.

Emergencies

Drivers are permitted to work outside the EU
rules as described above when an emergency
arises, but only by as much as is necessary to
enable them to reach a suitable stopping place
and provided that road safety is not jeopardized.

For these purposes an emergency is an
event where action is necessary to ensure the
safety of:

- persons;
- the vehicle; or
- its load.

The nature of and reasons for exceeding the
rules in these circumstances must be noted on
the driver's tachograph chart.

Prohibition on certain payments

The EU rules prohibit any payment to wage-
earning drivers in the form of bonuses or wage
supplements related to distances travelled
and/or the amount of goods carried, unless
such payments do not endanger road safety.

Enforcement and penalties

The driving hours rules are applied for reasons of public safety, in particular to protect road users from the dangers of overworked and tired drivers being in control of heavy vehicles. They are enforced vigorously by both the police and by VOSA enforcement officers, with convicted offenders being dealt with very severely by the courts to emphasize the importance with which these road safety measures are viewed.

Drivers who contravene the rules as described in this chapter can expect to be prosecuted if caught and fined heavily by the courts on conviction – the most serious of such offences can result in imprisonment – and those who hold LGV driving entitlements may find these, and thus possibly their job, in jeopardy.

Besides prosecution for infringements and its consequent penalties, under new provisions brought in by the Transport Act 2000 (ie section 266 which amends section 99 of the Transport Act 1968) effective from 1 February 2001, enforcement officers of the Vehicle Inspectorate have powers to detain drivers found to be in breach of the drivers' hours rules.

Where it is determined during a roadside check that a UK driver has not taken sufficient break or rest periods prior to that time, the driver will be prohibited from continuing his or her journey. In the case of break period infringements the delay at the roadside will be until a full 45-minute break period has been taken. Where breaches of the daily or weekly rest period requirements are detected, the driver and his or her vehicle will be escorted by the police to a suitable parking area (eg service area or truck stop) where the driver will have to remain until he or she has taken a full 11-hour daily rest or 24-hour weekly rest.

The vehicle operator may send a relief driver to take over the vehicle and continue its journey, but this driver will be subjected to scrutiny by the VI to ensure that he or she has sufficient time available within legal limits to drive the vehicle.

Employers of convicted drivers also risk prosecution and heavy fines for similar offences. Additionally they may have penalties imposed against their 'O' licences by the Traffic Commissioners (TCs) since they promised in the declaration of intent at the time of their 'O' licence application that they would make arrangements to ensure the drivers' hours law would be observed.

It is also a specific requirement of the EU rules that employers must make periodic checks to ensure the rules are observed and must take appropriate action if they discover breaches of the law to ensure there is no repetition of offences.

On the continent, breaches of the rules detected in roadside checks may result in drivers incurring heavy on-the-spot fines which must be paid immediately, otherwise the vehicle may be impounded and the driver held until the fine is paid.

Reporting of illegal operations

Under the Public Interest Disclosure Act 1998, employees are protected if they report corruption, wrongdoing or danger at work, or if they are unduly pressured by an unscrupulous employer to break the law.

For example, in the context of this Guide, where drivers are encouraged or pressured to break either the driving hours or tachograph rules, they would have protection under the Act if they reported such matters either to the Vehicle Inspectorate or to the Traffic Commissioner.

This so-called 'whistle-blowing' charter entitles workers to unlimited compensation if their employer penalizes them for exposing breaches of the law or unsafe practices.

Besides this legal protection, the United Road Transport Union (URTU) provides a confidential hotline service for drivers on freephone 0800 526639.

Revision of the EU driving hours rules

The European Council of Transport Ministers has been discussing proposals for amendment to the current EU driving hours regulation (3820/85/EC) which came into force on 29 September 1986. In September 2003 the following amendments were proposed, but it should be noted that these changes must be approved by the EU Council of Ministers before any final decisions are made:

- It is proposed to extend the regulations to include vehicles over 2.8 tonnes involved in international point-to-point delivery services.
- The definition of a fixed week will remain unchanged as 00.00 hours Monday to 24.00 hours Sunday.
- The normal daily rest period requirement will be increased to 12 hours with reduced rest periods of at least 9 hours available three times per week (ie between any two weekly rest periods). There will be no requirement to 'compensate' for reduced rest as at present.

- The daily rest period may be split into two uninterrupted periods of 3 hours each plus a 9-hour rest in a 24-hour period.
- The present facility for reducing weekly rest to 36 hours when taken at base or 24 hours if taken away from base will remain, but reductions will need to be compensated by the end of the following week.
- Reduced weekly rest periods while away from base can be taken in vehicles provided they have suitable sleeping facilities.
- Changes to the rest requirements will allow weekly rest to be taken at the start of one week, with the next weekly rest required at the end of the following week (potentially allowing 14 consecutive working days).
- Driving on and off road will all count towards the maximum driving limits except that driving *solely* off road (ie 'on-site' only) will not count as driving time.
- The maximum weekly driving limit will be 56 hours while fortnightly driving will remain at a maximum of 90 hours as now.
- On any day when driving a vehicle to which EU rules apply, driving time in any other goods vehicle, including light vans, will count toward the daily and weekly driving total.
- There will be an exemption for drivers of breakdown vehicles operating within a 100-kilometre radius of their base.
- Derogation will be granted for vehicles not exceeding 7.5 tonnes that are used to deliver postal items as part of the universal service within a 50-kilometre radius of base.
- At roadside checks, drivers will be required to produce records for the current day plus those for the 15 previous consecutive days.

- Consignors, freight forwarders, prime contractors, sub-contractors and driver employment agencies will be required to ensure that contractually agreed transport time schedules respect the provision of the regulations.
- It will be necessary for the compulsory downloading of data from digital tachographs at a frequency determined by individual member states.
- Drivers will be required to make manual entries on record sheets and digital equipment for periods they spend away from their vehicle.

Acknowledgement: This information was taken from the Freight Transport Association Web site: www.fta.co.uk.

AETR RULES

Drivers on international journeys beyond the European Union that take them to or through the list of countries given below are required to observe what are commonly known and referred to as the AETR rules. AETR stands for the European Agreement Concerning the Work of Crews of Vehicles Engaged in International Road Transport – 1971.

When on such journeys, the driver must observe the AETR rules for the whole of the outward and return journey, including the portion travelled in Britain and through other EU member states. However, these rules are now fully harmonized with the EU rules (contained in EC Regulation 3820/85 – since 1992) as described in this chapter, so in effect the driver need take no action beyond complying fully with the normal EU rules.

The countries beyond the EU referred to above where the AETR rules apply (ie on journeys to or through these countries) are as follows:

Belarus	the Czech Republic	Poland
Bosnia	Estonia	Romania
Bulgaria	Latvia	Slovakia
the CIS	Moldova	Slovenia
Croatia	Norway	Yugoslavia

2

FITMENT AND USE OF TACHOGRAPHS

INTRODUCTION

Tachograph instruments installed in goods vehicles provide a means of recording time and the speed and distance travelled by the vehicle. This record enables drivers' working activities and driving practices to be monitored to ensure that legal requirements – especially the drivers' hours rules – have been met.

The fitment of tachographs and their use in goods vehicles operating under the EU driving hours rules (see Chapter 1) for record-keeping purposes originally became a legal requirement in the UK on 31 December 1981. EU Regulation 3821/85/EC, which came into effect on 29 September 1986, amended some of the original requirements.

A new generation of digital tachographs is being introduced from 2005 (see Chapter 9).

WHICH VEHICLES REQUIRE TACHOGRAPHS?

The law requires the fitment and use of tachographs in most goods vehicles and other vehicles used for the carriage of goods that are over 3.5 tonnes permissible maximum weight (pmw), with certain EU exemptions as listed in the Appendix.

It is important to note that, unless a vehicle is used for purely private purposes only or is specifically exempted as shown by the exemptions list, the law applies; this means to:

- any goods vehicle over 3.5 tonnes pmw, or a combination of a goods vehicle and goods-carrying trailer which together are over 3.5 tonnes permissible maximum weight; and
- any other vehicle (such as off-road jeep-type vehicles, and 4 × 4s) used for the carriage of goods which when towing a trailer has a combined permissible maximum weight of more than 3.5 tonnes.

In particular, it should be noted that there is no exemption for short distance operations, infrequent-use vehicles or occasional driving – once a relevant vehicle is on the public highway (ie any road to which the public has access – and that includes public car parks and so-called private dock roads) the law applies in full (see also page 6).

WHAT THE LAW REQUIRES

Where the law applies as described above, a tachograph instrument must be installed in the vehicle and whoever drives that vehicle must produce a tachograph record and comply with the EU drivers' hours law, in full, both for:

- the day on which the driving takes place; and
- the week in which that day falls.

Under the EU regulations a number of specific requirements relating to tachograph use must be met as follows:

- The tachograph instrument must conform to the technical specification laid down in EU Regulation 3821/85/EC (as amended by Regulation 2479/95/EC – see below).
- The instrument must be calibrated and officially sealed at an approved calibration centre to ensure that accurate (ie legally acceptable) records are made (see page 56).
- The instrument must be used in accordance with the regulations, with individual responsibilities being observed by both employer and driver.

Amending Regulation 2479/95/EC demands the fitment of so-called 'tough' tachographs as follows:

Figure 2.1 Typical tachograph instrument. Courtesy: Kienzle VDO

- Electronic tachographs must be capable of detecting interruptions in the power supply.
- Driving time must be recorded automatically.
- Facilities must be provided for the removal and subsequent refitting, by an approved centre, of recording equipment seals to enable speed limiters to be fitted.
- Cables connecting electronic tachographs to the transmitter (ie sender unit) must be protected by a continuous steel sheath (ie a tamper-proof armoured cable).

EXEMPTIONS

There is no requirement for the fitment and use of tachographs in the types of vehicles described below or in vehicles used in connection with the particular transport operations shown in the exemptions list in the Appendix.

NB: It should be noted that the tachograph exemptions list is fundamentally the same as that for the EU hours law under Regulation 3820/85/EC.

However, vehicles that are exempt from the tachograph rules are not necessarily exempt from record-keeping requirements. For example, drivers of vehicles operating under the British domestic hours rules as described in Chapter 4 must keep written (logbook) records in accordance with Chapter 5.

Under amendments to the tachograph rules effective from 24 August 1998 under the Community Drivers' Hours and Recording Equipment (Amendment) Regulations 1998, tachograph fitment requirements now apply to vehicles which are not in themselves considered to be goods vehicles (eg four-wheel-drive off-road jeep-type vehicles) and which previously were exempt from the rules.

When such vehicles are drawing a trailer for the carriage of goods for commercial purposes, and the combined weight of the towing vehicle and the trailer exceeds 3.5 tonnes, the fitment and use of tachographs as described in this chapter is necessary and the driver must observe the EU drivers' hours law as set out in Chapter 1.

Declaration of exemption

When presenting a vehicle for the goods vehicle annual test which the operator believes is exempt from the tachograph regulations in accordance with the list above, a 'Declaration of Exemption' form has to be completed.

EMPLOYERS' RESPONSIBILITIES

It is the legal responsibility of the driver's employer to determine whether his or her transport operation and vehicles fall within the EU tachograph requirements. He or she does this by referring to the exemptions list in the Appendix to see if the operation is listed as being exempt from the rules:

- If it is listed as being exempt, the employer should refer to Chapters 4 and 5 to see what further action he or she may need to take to comply with the British domestic hours and record-keeping rules.
- If it is not listed as being exempt, the employer should take appropriate steps regarding the fitment and calibration of tachographs as described in this chapter. He

or she must also instruct his or her drivers accordingly in their use.

Additionally, the regulations place specific responsibilities on the employer of a driver who drives within the EU rules. He or she must:

- organize the driver's work in such a way that both the driver's hours and tachograph rules are complied with;
- supply drivers with sufficient numbers of the correct type of tachograph charts, ie:
  - one chart for the day,
  - one spare in case the first is impounded by an enforcement officer,
  - plus any further spares which are necessary to account for any charts which become too dirty or damaged to use;
- ensure that completed charts are collected from drivers no later than 21 days after use;
- periodically check completed charts to ensure that the law has been complied with, ie that:
  - the driver has made a chart for the day,
  - he or she has completed it fully and properly, and
  - he or she has observed the driving hours rules;
- take appropriate steps to prevent repetition of any breaches of the law that are found;
- retain completed charts for 12 months for inspection by Vehicle Inspectorate (VI) examiners, if required; and
- give copies of their records (ie charts) to any driver who requests them.

A number of court cases have highlighted the extent of employer responsibilities for tachograph operation as follows:

- It has been made clear that employers who do not check tachograph records are permitting drivers' hours offences and can be prosecuted and convicted accordingly.
- Employers can be charged with failing to use the tachograph in accordance with the regulations in cases where a driver is unable to produce charts to show his or her driving and other work activities when requested to do so in a roadside check.
- Where employers allow drivers to take their vehicle, or just the tractive unit, home after the day's work they must ensure that such driving is recorded on a tachograph chart and is counted as part of the driver's legally permitted driving and working time for that day – it is not part of his or her rest period.

DRIVERS' RESPONSIBILITIES

Responsibility for the correct (ie legal) use of tachographs rests with the driver who must fully understand what the law requires of him or her in this respect. This means that the driver has a legal duty to understand what the law requires and how to comply with it.

Drivers must ensure that the tachograph instrument in their vehicle functions correctly throughout the whole of their working shift to allow a full and proper recording for a full 24 hours to be produced. They must also ensure that they have sufficient quantities of the right type of charts on which to make recordings.

Not knowing what the law requires or how to comply with it are not acceptable excuses to be put forward in defence of a prosecution for tachograph offences. The courts will take the view that it is the driver's duty to know these things.

The specific responsibilities of drivers in regard to tachograph law are as follows:

- They must ensure that a proper record is made by the instrument, ie that:
  - it is a continuous record, and
  - it is a 'time right' record (ie recordings are in the correct 12-hour section of the chart – daytime or night-time hours).
- If the tachograph fails, or when no tachograph-fitted vehicle is available, while the driver is working he or she must make manual recordings of his or her activities on the chart – these must be legible and must not dirty the chart.
- They must produce for inspection on request by an authorized inspecting officer:
  - a current chart for that day,
  - charts relating to the current week, and
  - a chart for the last day of the previous week in which they drove.
- They must return completed charts to their employer no later than 21 days after use.
- They must allow any authorized inspecting officer to inspect the charts they have with them and the tachograph calibration plaque which is usually fixed inside the body of the instrument. This means allowing the officer into the vehicle cab where necessary.
- When they take their vehicle (or just the tractive unit) home at the end of their working shift, this time must be recorded on the tachograph chart and counted as part of the daily maximum driving time and their day's work – it is not part of their rest period.

TWO-CREW OPERATION (DOUBLE-MANNING)

Reference to a driver also includes any other driver who is carried on the vehicle to assist with the driving (as with double manning). In this case a two-person tachograph must be fitted to the vehicle and both drivers must use it simultaneously to produce records as follows:

- The person who is driving must have his or her chart located in the uppermost (ie number 1) position in the instrument and use the number 1 activity mode switch to enable his or her activities and vehicle speed and distance recordings to be made on the chart as appropriate.
- The person who is riding passenger must have his or her chart in the rearmost (ie number 2) position and must use the number 2 activity mode switch to record his or her other work activities, or break or rest periods. Only time group recordings are made on this chart; driving, speed and distance traces are *not* produced on the second-person chart.

NB: Following a High Court ruling it is clear that the second person on a double-manned vehicle must insert his or her chart in the second-person position of the instrument from the start of the journey, not from the later time when he or she commences his or her period of driving.

TACHOGRAPH BREAKDOWN

If tachograph equipment becomes defective (or the seals are broken for whatever reason, including authorized breakage, as described above, to carry out mechanical repairs to the vehicle, or unauthorized interference), it must be repaired at an approved centre as soon as 'circumstances permit', but in the meantime the driver must continue to record manually on the chart all necessary information regarding his or her working, driving, breaks and rest times which are no longer being recorded by the instrument. There is *no* requirement to attempt to record speed or distance.

Once a vehicle has returned to base with a defective tachograph, it should not leave again until the instrument is in working order and has been re-calibrated (if necessary) and the seals replaced. If it cannot be repaired immediately, the vehicle can be used so long as the operator has taken positive steps (which he or she can satisfactorily prove later if challenged by the enforcement authorities – see paragraph below) to have the installation repaired as soon as reasonably practicable.

If a vehicle is unable to return to base within *one week* (ie seven days), counting from the day of the breakdown, arrangements must be made to have the defective instrument repaired and re-calibrated as necessary at an approved centre *en route* within that time.

Defence

There is a defence in the regulations against conviction (ie not against prosecution) for an offence of using a vehicle with a defective tachograph. This has the effect of allowing subsequent use of a vehicle with a defective tachograph provided steps have been taken to have the installation restored to a legal condition as soon as circumstances permit and provided the driver continues to record his or her driving, working and break period times manually on a tachograph chart. In such circumstances it will be necessary to satisfactorily prove to the enforcement authorities – and to the court if they proceed with prosecution – that a definite booking for the repair had already been made at the time the vehicle was apprehended and that this appointment was for the repair to be carried out at the earliest possible opportunity.

It is also a defence to show that at the time it was examined by an enforcement officer the vehicle was on its way to an approved tachograph centre to have necessary repairs carried out. However, this defence will fail if the driver did not keep written records of his or her activities in the meantime.

TIME CHANGES

Drivers must ensure that the time at which the instrument clock is set and consequently recordings are made on the chart agree with the official time in the country of registration of the vehicle.

This is a significant point for British drivers travelling in Europe who may be tempted to change the clock in the instrument to the correct local European time rather than, for example, having it indicate and record the time in Britain.

To re-emphasize the point, this means that for British drivers in British-registered vehicles the tachograph chart recording must accord with the official time in Britain regardless of the country in which that recording was made – the tachograph clock must *not* be reset to show local time when travelling abroad.

DIRTY OR DAMAGED CHARTS

If a chart becomes dirty or damaged in use, it must be replaced and the old chart should be securely attached to the new chart that is used to replace it.

COMPLETION OF THE CHART CENTRE FIELD

Before starting work with a vehicle in which tachograph charts are to be used, the driver must enter on the centre field of his or her chart for that day the following details:

- his or her surname and first name (not initials);
- the date and place where use of the chart begins;
- vehicle registration number;
- the distance recorder (odometer) reading at the start of the day.

At the end of a working day, the driver should then record the following information on the chart:

- the place and date where the chart is completed;
- the closing odometer reading;
- by subtraction, the total distance driven – in kilometres.

MAKING RECORDINGS

When the centre field has been completed the chart should be inserted in the tachograph

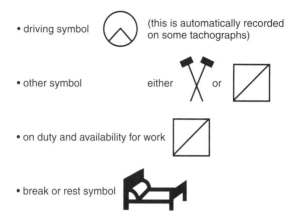

Figure 2.2 Symbols

instrument, ensuring that it is the right way up (it should be impossible to fit it wrongly) and that the recording will commence on the correct part of the 24-hour chart (day or night). The instrument face should be securely closed.

The activity mode switch (number 1) should be turned as necessary throughout the work period to indicate the driver's relevant activities, namely driving, other work, break or rest periods. While some drivers find difficulty in getting into the habit of turning the switch to coincide with each change of activity, nevertheless this is what the law requires and it is an offence to fail to do so (ie a charge of not keeping proper records).

Other work and overtime recordings

The High Court has ruled that drivers must record *all* periods of work on their tachograph charts. This makes it clear that work undertaken for the employer after the daily driving shift has been completed (eg in a yard, warehouse, workshop or office), and whether deemed part of the normal day or overtime working, must be recorded on the chart for that day – ie either by the instrument if this is convenient or otherwise manually.

A contention that since tachographs were intended primarily to record driving time in the interests of road safety they should be used for that purpose only and not for recording other working activities was ruled to be contrary to the provisions of both the EU legislation and section 97 of the Transport Act 1968.

Overnight recordings

At the end of his or her shift the driver can leave the chart in the instrument overnight to record the daily rest period or alternatively it can be removed and the rest period recorded manually on the chart.

Generally, enforcement officers prefer an automatic recording of daily rest made by the instrument, but this is not always practicable where the vehicle may be:

- used by other drivers on night-shift work;
- driven for road testing or other purposes by workshop staff; or
- moved around the premises by others when the driver is taking his or her statutory rest period.

Also, if the driver is scheduled to start work later on the following day, if he or she leaves the chart in the tachograph overnight there will be an overlap recording on the chart which is illegal.

Vehicle changes

If drivers change to another vehicle during the working day they must take the existing chart with them and record:

- details of the time of change;
- the registration number of the further vehicle(s); and
- distance recordings in the appropriate spaces on the chart.

They then use that chart in the next vehicle to record their continuing driving, working activities and break periods. This procedure is repeated no matter how many different vehicles (except those not driven on the public highway) are driven during the day so the one chart shows (where possible) all of the driver's daily activity – but see also below.

Mixed tachographs

It is important to note that the various makes and models of tachograph currently available in the UK have different charts and they cannot all be interchanged – albeit some 'universal charts' are available. So the driver who switches from a vehicle with one make of instrument to a vehicle with a different make during the working day will have to make fresh entries on a second or even third chart.

At the end of the day all the charts used should be attached together to present a comprehensive (and legal) record for the whole day.

It is the employer's duty to issue drivers with the correct charts (ie with matching type approval numbers to those on the tachograph instrument in use) in sufficient numbers for the schedule that the driver has to operate.

MANUAL RECORDS

Drivers are responsible for ensuring that the instrument is kept running while they are in charge of the vehicle and should it fail or otherwise cease making proper records they should remove the chart and continue to record their activities manually on it as previously described. They must also make manual recordings on the chart of work done or time spent away from the vehicle (for example, periods during the day spent working in the yard, warehouse or workshop). Manual recordings must be made legibly and in making them the sheet must not be dirtied or damaged and existing recordings made by the tachograph must not be defaced.

RECORDS FOR PART-TIME DRIVERS

The rules on the use of tachographs described in the foregoing text apply equally to part-time or occasional drivers such as yard and warehouse staff, office people and even the transport manager. The rules also apply fully even if the driving on the road is for a very short distance or period of time – a five-minute drive without a tachograph chart in use would be sufficient to break the law and risk prosecution.

Vehicle fitters and other workshop staff who drive vehicles on the road for testing purposes in connection with repair or maintenance are specifically exempt from the need to keep tachograph records when undertaking such activities (see exemptions list in the Appendix), but this exemption *does not* apply to them when using vehicles for other purposes (eg collecting spare parts, ferrying vehicles back and forth, taking replacement vehicles out to on-road breakdowns, taking and collecting vehicles to and from goods vehicle test stations etc).

RETENTION, RETURN AND CHECKING OF TACHOGRAPH CHARTS

Drivers must retain and be able to produce, on request by authorized examiners (including the police), completed tachograph charts for each driving day of the current week and for the last day of the previous week on which they drove. Charts do not have to be made for non-driving or rest days and the police therefore cannot ask for charts in respect of such days.

Drivers must return charts to their employer no later than 21 days after use and, on receiving the charts, the employer must periodically check them to ensure that the drivers' hours and record-keeping regulations have been complied with.

Failure by an operator to check charts for possible offences by drivers can lead to charges of 'permitting' certain tachograph and drivers' hours offences (should such offences be proven) – in one case a transport manager was held to be 'reckless' because his chart checking system was not sufficiently thorough.

Charts must be retained, available for inspection if required, for a period of one year.

More than one employer

Where drivers have more than one employer in a week, as may be the case where they are agency drivers, they must return the tachograph charts to the employer who first employed them in that week. From the employer's point of view this provision clearly presents a problem where agency drivers are regularly employed – they may find difficulty in obtaining charts relating to driving work done with their vehicles.

Retention of charts for tax records

Where tachograph charts are used by employers to justify payment of driver night-out and other subsistence expenses for tax purposes, the charts constitute part of the legal recording system for tax purposes and as such must be retained for six years instead of the normal one-year period as described above.

OFFICIAL INSPECTION OF CHARTS

An authorized inspecting officer (which means a traffic examiner of the Vehicle Inspectorate or a person authorized by a Traffic Commissioner (TC), in either case on production of their authority if requested, or a police officer) may require any person to produce for inspection any tachograph chart on which recordings have been made. These charts are analysed for contraventions of the law.

Further, the examiner may enter a vehicle (see note below) to inspect a chart or a tachograph instrument (he or she should be able to read the recordings relating to the nine hours prior to the time of his or her inspection) and the calibration plaques. The examiner may actually detain a stationary vehicle for this purpose – but only a police officer can stop a moving vehicle.

At any reasonable time an examiner may enter premises on which he or she believes vehicles or tachograph charts are kept and inspect the instruments in such vehicles and the completed charts. He or she can require, by serving a notice in writing, charts to be produced at a Traffic Area Office at any time on giving at least 10 days' notice in which to do so.

Where a chart is suspected of showing a false entry, an examiner may 'seize' the chart (but not for reasons other than evidence of a false entry, or an entry intended to deceive, or an entry altered for such purposes) and retain it for a maximum period of six months, after which time, if no charges for offences have been made, the chart should be returned. If it is not returned voluntarily or willingly, the person from whom it was taken can apply to a magistrate's court to seek an order for its return.

In practice, VI examiners regularly ask operators to provide batches of tachograph charts covering one or more of their vehicles for a short period or possibly some months either on a routine basis or following investigations into, or leads about, drivers' hours law or tachograph infringements – and where it is suspected that drivers are regularly exceeding speed limits.

The courts have ruled that examiners do have powers to remove tachograph charts from operators' premises when acting on the instructions of a TC – this follows the successful prosecution of a haulage firm that refused to allow charts to be removed from its premises.

Cases have been reported where the police have demanded that operators should send in to them, by post, tachograph charts required for inspection. This has been shown to be an illegal practice: there is no provision in the law that allows random collection of charts by the police or demands for charts to be submitted by post. Only in cases where an on-the-spot examination reveals possible offences can the police then request copies of the relevant chart for that day, other charts for that week and for the last day of the previous week. Vehicle Inspectorate enforcement officers, on the other hand, may take random selections of charts away for examination.

It is an offence to fail to produce records for inspection as required or to obstruct an enforcement officer in his or her request to inspect records or tachograph installations in vehicles.

OFFENCES

Some tachograph-related offences have already been mentioned in connection with specific requirements of the law but there are other overriding, and very serious, offences to be considered. In particular, it is an offence:

- to use, cause or permit the use of a vehicle which does not have a fully calibrated tachograph installed;
- for the driver to fail to keep records by means of a tachograph (or manually if the instrument is defective); and
- to make false recordings.

Further, it is an offence for the driver to fail to:

- return used charts to his or her employer within 21 days after use; or
- notify his or her first employer of any other employer for whom he or she drives vehicles to which the regulations apply.

In many cases offences committed by the driver result in charges against the employer for 'causing' or 'permitting' offences. For example, where tachograph charts go missing and cannot be produced for examination by the enforcement authorities, the employer may be charged with any one of three (or even all three) relevant offences, namely:

- failing to cause the driver to keep a record;
- failing to preserve the record;
- failing to produce the record.

It is in such cases that sound legal representation should be sought and a good defence put forward where possible.

Two other types of offence that have featured in extensively reported prosecutions concern:

- missing mileages when charts are compared;
- interference with tachograph systems by various means of wires and so-called 'magic buttons'.

PENALTIES

Penalties on summary conviction for offences under these regulations can be a fine of up to level 4 on the standard scale (currently £2,500) and conviction for such offences can jeopardize both the employer's 'O' licence and the driver's LGV driving entitlement.

Conviction for the more serious offences of making false entries on a tachograph chart and forgery can result in level 5 fines of up to £5,000 (per offence) or imprisonment for up to two years.

Since 1 April 1998 tachograph falsification has been a 'recordable' offence, meaning that a person convicted of such an offence carries a criminal record.

Traffic Commissioners have made it clear that heavy goods drivers convicted for using wires to interfere with their tachograph will be disqualified from holding an LGV driving licence for a period of one year.

Much heavier penalties are likely for those transport operators and LGV drivers found guilty in UK courts of forging tachograph charts and making false entries on charts relating to international journeys. These penalties are contained in the provisions of the Forgery and Counterfeiting Act 1981 which the Court of Appeal now allows the police to use for bringing prosecutions for tachograph chart offences committed outside the UK. Fines may be in excess of the current level 5 standard scale maximum of £5,000, and custodial sentences could be longer than those available to the courts under other legislation.

The courts have ruled that in cases where a driver or transport operator claims not to have known that the tachograph instrument in a vehicle had been fitted with a device intended to interfere with its operation (ie a trip device to aid the production of false records), this was no excuse and an offence of 'strict liability' was committed to which there is no defence.

OFFICIAL EXAMINATION OF TACHOGRAPH CHARTS

Under EU Regulation 3821/85/EEC an authorized inspecting officer may require a driver to produce record sheets for the current week and the last day of the previous week on which he or she drove a vehicle within scope of the driving hours regulations (ie 3820/85/EEC).

An 'authorized inspecting officer' includes police officers and VI examiners authorized under Section 99 of the Transport Act 1968 to examine records. Under this section a policeman, a VI examiner or a person authorized by a Traffic Commissioner may, on production of his or her authority if it is requested (except that police officers in uniform do not have to produce an authority), ask any person to produce and permit him or her to inspect and copy:

- any book or register which that person is required under Section 98 (ie record books for drivers on national work exempt the EC rules) to carry or have in his or her possession;
- any book or register as in (a) which that person is required to preserve;
- any record sheet the person is required under EC tachograph rules to retain or be able to produce;
- if the person is the owner of a vehicle to which the hours and records law applies, any other document which the official may reasonably require to inspect to check that the law is being complied with;
- any book, register or other document required to be kept by the EC rules or which the officer may reasonably require to inspect to check that the EC hours and records rules are being complied with.

A police officer or authorized examiner can also require, by written notice, that any record sheet, book, register or other document referred to above, shall be produced at the office of the

Traffic Commissioner by a specified time, but not within 10 days of the notice.

In acting under the first and last items in the list above, an officer can detain a vehicle during the time required for inspecting and copying records and record books.

Section 99 states that an officer may, at any time that is reasonable in the circumstances, enter any premises on which he or she has reason to believe that a goods vehicle is kept or any record sheet, books, registers or other documents are to be found, and inspect any such vehicle and inspect, and copy, any record sheet, book, register or any other document he or she finds there.

Section 99(6) gives an officer power to seize any record sheet that he or she has reasonable cause to believe is false or has been altered with intent to deceive.

Under Section 19(2) of the Police and Criminal Evidence Act 1984, a police officer (but not a VI examiner) who is lawfully on the premises (including a place or a vehicle) has power to seize anything which is on the premises if he or she has reasonable grounds for believing that:

- it is evidence in relation to an offence which he or she is investigating or any other offence; and
- it is necessary to seize it in order to prevent the evidence being concealed, lost, altered or destroyed.

CHART ANALYSIS

Analysis of the information recorded on tachograph charts can provide valuable data for determining whether drivers have complied with the law on driving, working, break and rest period times and have conformed to statutory speed limits.

The chart data can also be extremely useful as a basis for increasing the efficiency of vehicle operations and for establishing productivity monitoring and payment schemes for drivers. It is also claimed that by detailed analysis of the charts and by keeping drivers aware of the information obtained, driving methods can be improved, thus saving fuel and cutting down on the wear and tear on vehicle brakes, tyres, transmission and other components.

The German company Siemens VDO Automotive AG (and its British subsidiary Siemens VDO Trading Limited of Birmingham), which is the leading tachograph manufacturer, has undertaken considerable research into chart analysis and is able to offer users the service of its analysis experts both in Germany and in the UK, as well as in other countries, to determine the activities of drivers and vehicles and particularly the progress of a vehicle immediately prior to an accident and at the point of impact. In some instances such analysis has shown that witnesses' accounts of the speed of the vehicle and its braking force just before the accident have been far from correct.

Use of chart analysis agencies

Many fleet operators use and rely upon the services of tachograph analysis agencies for checking their charts for conformity with the law. However, it should be noted that should such firms fail to recognize and notify the operator of deficiencies in their records, it is the operator who is at risk, and his or her licence put in jeopardy, not the analysis bureau. Traffic

Commissioners repeatedly remind operators that responsibility for driver compliance with the hours law rests entirely with them, not with outside agencies.

Generally also, it should be noted that the checking carried out by agencies is for standard hours law infringements only, which are mainly picked up by computerized analysis and may not include identification of other irregularities or cleverly executed false entries or fraudulent recordings. Similarly, such analysis may not identify driver abuse of vehicles or frequent and excessive speeding.

Chart analysis equipment

The leading tachograph manufacturers supply suitable equipment to enable detailed chart analysis to be carried out by transport operators. A chart analyser magnifies the used chart to the extent that detailed analysis beyond the scope of a normal visual examination can be made of the vehicle's minute-by-minute and kilometre-by-kilometre progress. Journey times, average running times and speeds, delivery times, route miles, traffic delays and many other relevant factors can be readily established. With the aid of a fixed hairline cursor on the magnifier to allow precise definition of the time and speed scales and recordings on the chart, even the vehicle's rates of acceleration and deceleration can be determined.

Tachograph charts as evidence

In the past, it has been made clear that tachograph charts, while providing evidence of 'the facts shown' for drivers' hours purposes, would not be used by the police and enforcement authorities as evidence to bring prosecutions against drivers for speeding offences – not to be confused with the Traffic Commissioner's actions in imposing short-term LGV driving bans on drivers found from their charts to have regularly exceeded maximum speed limits.

However, it has been mooted that the law may be changed in the future to permit the retrospective checking of tachograph charts for speeding and prosecution of drivers where such evidence is shown. This follows publicity surrounding a number of serious coach and lorry crashes where speeding was thought to be a contributory factor.

Tachograph chart fiddles

A key feature of tachograph recordings is that careful observation will show results of the majority of faults in recordings as well as fiddles and attempts at falsification of recordings by drivers. The main faults likely to be encountered will show as follows:

- Clock stops – recordings continue in a single vertical line until the styli penetrate the chart.
- Styli jam/seize up – recordings continue around the chart with no vertical movement.
- Cable or electronic drive failure – chart continues to rotate and speed and distance styli continue to record on baseline and where last positioned, respectively. Time group recordings can still be made but no driving trace will appear.

Attempts at falsification of charts will appear as follows:

- Opening the instrument face will result in a gap in recordings.

- Winding the clock backwards or forwards will leave either a gap in the recording or an overlap. In either case the distance recording will not match up if the vehicle is moved.
- Stopping the clock will stop the rotation of the chart, so all speed and distance recordings will be on one vertical line (see items listed on previous page about how faults in instruments show on charts).
- Restricting the speed stylus to give indications of lower than actual speed will result in flat-topped speed recordings, while bending the stylus down to achieve the same effect will result in recordings below the speed baseline when the vehicle is stationary.
- Written or marked-in recordings with pens or sharp pointed objects are readily identifiable by even a relatively unskilled chart analyst.

This is only an outline list of a large number of possible faults and attempts at falsification likely to be encountered. Some driver fiddles are one-off attempts, crudely and clumsily executed and naively obvious; others are much more sophisticated in their execution, often as part of an ongoing violation of legal requirements. These are more difficult, but not impossible, for the transport manager or fleet operator to detect and would certainly be picked up quickly by an experienced chart analyst.

3

TACHOGRAPHS, RECORDINGS AND CALIBRATION

THE TACHOGRAPH INSTRUMENT

A tachograph is a cable or electronically driven speedometer incorporating an integral electric clock and a chart recording mechanism. It is fitted into the vehicle dashboard or in some other convenient visible position in the driving cab. The instrument indicates time, speed and distance and permanently records this information on the chart as well as the driver's working activities. Thus, the following factors can be determined from a chart:

- varying speeds (and the highest speed) at which the vehicle was driven;
- total distance travelled and distances between individual stops;
- times when the vehicle was being driven and the total amount of driving time;
- times when the vehicle was standing and whether the driver was indicating other work, break or rest period during this time.

RECORDINGS

Recordings are made on special circular charts, each of which covers a period of 24 hours, by three styli as follows:

- one stylus records distance;
- the second stylus records speed; and
- the third stylus records time-group activities as determined by the driver turning the activity mode switch on the head of the instrument (ie to show driving, other work, breaks and rest periods).

The styli press through a wax recording layer on the chart, revealing the carbonated layer (usually black) between the top surface and the backing paper. The charts are accurately pre-marked with time, distance and speed reference radials and when the styli have marked the chart with the appropriate recordings these can be easily identified and interpreted against the printed reference marks:

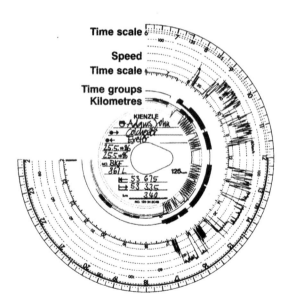

Figure 3.1 A typical tachograph chart showing recordings of time, distance and speed

- Movement of the vehicle creates a broad running line on the time radial, indicating when the vehicle started running and when it stopped. After the vehicle has stopped, the time-group stylus continues to mark the chart but with an easily distinguishable thin line.
- The speed trace gives an accurate recording of the speeds attained at all times throughout the journey, continuing to record on the speed baseline when the vehicle is stationary to provide an unbroken trace except when the instrument is opened.
- The distance recording is made by the stylus moving up and down over a short stroke, each movement representing five kilometres travelled; thus, every five kilometres the stylus reverses direction, forming a 'V' for every 10 kilometres of distance travelled. To calculate the total distance covered, the 'V's are counted and multiplied by 10 and any 'tail ends' are added in, the total being expressed in kilometres.

When a second chart is located in the rear position of a two-person tachograph, only a time recording of the second person's activities (ie other work, break or rest) is shown. Traces showing driving, vehicle speed or distance cannot be recorded on this chart.

Precautions against interference with the readings are incorporated in the instrument. It is opened with a key and a security mark is made on the chart every time the instrument is opened.* When checking the chart it can be easily established at what time the instrument was opened and thus whether this was for an authorized reason or not. Interference with the recording mechanism to give false readings, particularly of speed, can be determined quite simply by an experienced chart analyst.

* NB: Changes to the EU tachograph specification to reduce the possibility of fraudulent recordings were introduced to apply to new instruments receiving Type Approval from 1991. These include provision for the chart to be marked at every interruption of the power supply (eg when a fuse is removed).

DETECTION OF TACHOGRAPH FAULTS AND FAILURES

Tachographs are generally robust instruments, but listed below are some of the faults that may occur:

- failure of the cable drive at the vehicle gearbox;
- failure of the cable drive at the tachograph head;
- failure of the adaptor/corrector/triplex gearbox;
- cable breaking or seizure;
- electrical faults affecting lights in the instrument or the clock;
- incorrect time showing on the 24-hour clock (eg day-shift work becomes shown against night hours on the charts);
- failure of the tachograph head;
- damage to the recording styli;
- failure of the distance recorder;
- damage to charts because of incorrect insertion.

EU INSTRUMENTS AND CHARTS

Tachographs may only be used for legal record-keeping purposes if they are type-approved and comply with the detailed EU specification. Such instruments have provision for indicating to the driver, without the instrument being opened, that a chart has been inserted and that a continuous recording is being made. They also provide for the driver to select, by an activity mode switch on the instrument, the type of recording that is being made. In the UK this must be one of the following:

- driving time;
- other work time;
- break and rest periods.

Two-person instruments are also provided with a means of simultaneously recording the activities of a second crewmember on a separate chart located in the rear position in the instrument.

The charts used for legal purposes must also be type-approved as indicated by the appropriate 'e' (ie European approval) markings printed on them. It is illegal to use non-approved charts or charts which are not approved for the specific type of instrument being used. Care should be taken that charts used have accurate time registration – cheap and non-type approved versions, which are illegal anyway, have been found in the past to be significantly inaccurate in the way they are printed, thus producing inaccurate and worthless records.

TACHOGRAPH CALIBRATION, SEALING AND INSPECTION

To enable the tachograph instrument to make legally acceptable records it must be:

- calibrated initially at an approved tachograph centre (see your local *Yellow Pages* telephone directory);
- inspected every two years subsequently; and
- fully re-calibrated every six years, or after repair at an approved centre.

Tachograph centres

The Vehicle Inspectorate (VI) approves tachograph centres, including:

- display of a standard sign;
- the technical equipment used in the centre;
- the staff and their training; and
- procedures for the installation, repair, inspection, calibration and sealing of tachographs.

Such centres must be approved to the BS 5750 Part 2 quality assurance standard before they can gain VI approval. No other workshops or individuals are permitted to carry out such work. The tachograph installation would no longer be capable of producing legally acceptable records if any repair work was carried out by unauthorized agents.

It is an offence for any unauthorized person to carry out work on tachograph installations. It is also an offence for a vehicle operator to obtain and use a tachograph instrument repaired by a firm that is not BS 5750 approved. Maximum fines of up to £5,000 may be imposed on conviction for such offences.

Calibration

The calibration process requires the vehicle to be presented to an approved tachograph centre:

- in normal road-going trim;
- complete with body and all fixtures;
- unladen; and
- with tyres complying with legal limits as to tread wear and inflated to manufacturer's recommended pressures.

The regulations specify the tolerances within which the tachograph installation must operate – valid for temperatures between 0° and 40° C as follows:

On bench test	On installation	In use
Speed ±3 kph	±4 kph	±6 kph
Distance ±1%	±2%	±4%

Time in all cases, ±2 minutes per day with a maximum of 10 minutes per 7 days.

NB: In the case of both speed and distance figures shown above, the tolerance is measured relative to the real speed and to the real distance of at least one kilometre.

Calibration plaques

When a tachograph has been installed in a vehicle and calibrated, the approved centre must fix, either inside the tachograph head or near to it on the vehicle dashboard in a visible position, a plaque giving details of:

- the approved centre;
- the 'turns count'; and
- the calibration date.

The plaque is sealed and must not be tampered with or the sealing tape removed. When an instrument is subjected to a two-year inspection or re-calibration, a new plaque must be fitted. If a vehicle is found on the road with an 'out-of-date' calibration plaque an offence will have been committed and prosecution may follow.

The normal sequence for plaques is that:

- one will show the initial calibration date;
- the next (two years later), which is fitted alongside the first plaque, will show the date of the two-year inspection; and
- a third plaque will show the second two-year inspection (ie four years after initial calibration).

After a further two years, a six-year re-calibration of the installation will be due and at this time all the previous plaques will be removed, the new calibration plaque will be fitted and the procedure described above starts again.

In between times, following certain repairs, a 'minor work' plaque may be fitted but this does not alter the sequence of dates for the two-year inspection and the six-year re-calibration plaques.

The two-year and six-year periods referred to above for inspections and calibrations are counted to the exact date, *not* to the end of the month in which that date falls.

Calibration and periodic inspection fees

Official (maximum) fees charged for tachograph calibration and periodic inspections are currently as follows:

Calibration (the official time for this task being 1.5 hours)	£37.50 plus VAT
Two-yearly inspection	£24.00 plus VAT

NB: These prices are exclusive of any replacement parts used.

SEALING OF TACHOGRAPHS

Tachograph installations are sealed after calibration or after the two-yearly inspections by the approved centre using their own individually coded official seal, the details of which are maintained on a register by the VI. The seals are of the customs type where a wire is passed through each of the connecting points between the vehicle and the tachograph itself and then a lead seal is squeezed tight on to the wire with special pliers that imprint the centre code number in the metal.

The purpose of sealing is to ensure that there is no tampering with the equipment or any of its drive mechanisms or cables which could either vary the recordings of time, speed or distance or inhibit the recording in any way. Such tampering is illegal and once seals are broken the installation no longer complies with the law and legally acceptable records cannot be made.

Besides the seals inside the instrument head, the following points are sealed:

- the installation plaque;
- the two ends of the link between the recording equipment and the vehicle;
- the adaptor itself and the point of its insertion into the circuit;
- the switch mechanism for vehicles with two or more axle ratios;
- the links joining the adaptor and the switch mechanism to the rest of the equipment;
- the casings of the instrument;

- any cover giving access to the means of adapting the constant of the recording equipment to the characteristic coefficient of the vehicle.

Seal breakage

There are occasions when certain of the seals have to be broken of necessity to carry out repairs to the vehicle and replacement of defective parts (eg the vehicle clutch or gearbox). The only seals that may be legally broken in these circumstances are as follows:

- those at the two ends of the link between the tachograph equipment and the vehicle;
- those between the adaptor (ie the tachograph drive gearbox) and the point of its insertion into the circuit;
- those at the links joining the adaptor and the switch mechanism (ie where the vehicle has a two-speed rear axle) to the rest of the equipment.

Seals may also be broken to allow the fitting of a statutory speed-limiter device, but the seals must be replaced, at an approved tachograph centre, within seven days.

While it is permitted to break the particular seals listed above for other authorized purposes (eg in connection with vehicle maintenance):

- a written record must be kept of the breakage and the reason for doing so; and
- the installation must be inspected or re-calibrated and fully sealed as soon as 'circumstances permit' and before the vehicle is used again.

It is illegal to remove any of the other seals and tampering with seals by drivers is tantamount to committing fraud. This means that the courts would consider that it was done for the purposes of making fraudulent records, which is an offence liable to lead to a prison sentence.

4

BRITISH DOMESTIC DRIVERS' HOURS

INTRODUCTION

The current British domestic drivers' hours rules
came into effect on 29 September 1986. The
relevant legal provisions are contained in the
1968 Transport Act to which a number of
subsequent amendments have been made.

Unlike the complexities of the EU rules,
the domestic rules are minimal in scope and
quite simple to understand, comprising only
limits on:

- daily driving; and
- daily duty.

WHICH DRIVERS AND VEHICLES?

The rules apply to goods vehicle drivers whose
activities are outside the scope of the EU rules
as described in Chapter 1. In other words, they
apply to vehicles and transport operations that
are specified in the EU exemptions list shown in
the Appendix.

It is important to emphasize that drivers
who are exempt from the EU rules, either
because their vehicle does not exceed 3.5

tonnes permissible maximum weight, or because the work on which they are employed is shown in the list of EU exemptions in the Appendix, must comply with the British domestic rules as set out below.

Important points to note

Drivers of light goods vehicles (ie not exceeding 3.5 tonnes permissible maximum weight) must still conform to the legal limits on maximum daily driving and maximum daily duty despite the fact that no records of driving or working times are required to be kept.

If a trailer is attached to a vehicle not exceeding 3.5 tonnes permissible maximum weight (which itself is exempt from the EU rules on account of its weight), thereby taking the combined weight to over 3.5 tonnes, then the EU rules must be followed as described in Chapter 1, unless it is exempt for other reasons – namely the nature of the operations on which it is engaged is shown in the EU exemptions list in the Appendix.

EXEMPTIONS AND CONCESSIONS

The British domestic rules apply to drivers of all goods vehicles that are exempt from the EU regulations as described earlier, but with the following further exceptions which are totally exempt from all hours rules control:

- armed forces;
- police and fire brigade services;
- driving off the public road system;
- driving for purely private purposes (ie not in connection with any trade or business).

Additionally, the British domestic rules do not apply:

- to a driver who on any day does not drive a relevant vehicle; or
- to a driver who on each day of the week does not drive a vehicle within these rules for more than four hours (note: this exemption *does not* apply to a driver whose activities fall within scope of the EU rules).

DEFINITIONS

For the purposes of the British domestic rules:

- Driving means time spent behind the wheel actually driving a goods vehicle. Driving on off-road sites and premises such as quarries, civil engineering and building sites and on agricultural and forestry land is counted as duty time, not driving time.
- Driving time is the maximum amount of time spent driving on roads to which the public has access.
- Duty time is the time a driver spends working for his or her employer and includes any work undertaken, including the driving of private motor cars, for example, which is not driving time for the purposes of the regulations. The daily duty limit does not apply on any day when a driver does not drive a goods vehicle.

SUMMARY OF BRITISH DOMESTIC RULES

Maximum daily driving:	10 hours
Maximum daily duty:	11 hours

Daily rest:
minimum of 13 hours
so as not to exceed
the daily 11-hour duty limit

UNLIMITED ACTIVITIES

Unlike under previous sets of rules, currently there are no specified limits or requirements in relation to the following:

- continuous duty;
- daily spread-over;
- weekly duty;
- breaks during day;
- weekly rest.

EMERGENCIES

The daily driving and duty limits specified above may be suspended when an emergency situation arises. This is defined as an event requiring immediate action to avoid:

- danger to life or health of one or more individuals or animals;
- serious interruption in the maintenance of essential public services for the supply of gas, water, electricity, drainage, or of telecommunications and postal services;
- serious interruption in the use of roads, railways, ports or airports; or
- damage to property.

The driver must enter details of the emergency on his or her record sheet when the statutory limits are exceeded.

LIGHT VEHICLE DRIVING

As explained above, drivers of light goods vehicles not exceeding 3.5 tonnes permissible maximum weight – as with drivers of other goods vehicles which fall within the scope of these rules – must observe the daily limits on driving (10 hours) and duty (11 hours). However, only the 10-hour daily driving limit applies when such vehicles are used:

- by doctors, dentists, nurses, midwives or vets;
- for any service of inspection, cleaning, maintenance, repair, installation or fitting;
- by a commercial traveller and carrying only goods used for soliciting orders;
- by an employee of the AA, the RAC or the RSAC;
- for the business of cinematography or of radio or television broadcasting.

MIXED EU AND BRITISH DRIVING

It is possible that a goods vehicle driver may be engaged on the same day or within the same week in transport operations that come within scope of both the EU drivers' hours rules and the British domestic hours rules. When such a situation arises the driver may choose to:

- conform strictly to the EU rules throughout the whole of the driving/working period; or
- take advantage of the more liberal British domestic rules where appropriate.

If the driver decides on the latter and thereby combines both British and EU rules, he or she must beware of the following points:

- Time spent driving under the EU rules cannot count as an off-duty period for the British rules.
- Time spent driving or on duty under the British rules cannot count as a break or rest period under the EU rules.
- Driving under the EU rules counts towards the driving and duty limits for the British rules.
- Where any EU rules' driving is done in a week, the driver must observe the EU daily and weekly rest period requirements for the whole of that week.

REVISION OF BRITISH DOMESTIC RULES

It is likely that the British domestic drivers' hours rules will eventually be phased out and drivers currently operating under their provisions will have to follow the full EU rules as described in Chapter 1. The government stated in the July 1998 White Paper, *New Deal for Transport*, its intention to publish a consultation paper seeking views on this subject. However, nothing further on this subject had been announced when this *Guide* closed for printing.

5

DOMESTIC RECORD KEEPING

INTRODUCTION

Where a goods vehicle is outside the scope of the EU rules as described previously, the British domestic drivers' hours rules apply (see Chapter 4) and the driver of such a vehicle is required to keep written records of his or her driving and working activities by means of a 'logbook' system.

To summarize the main record-keeping alternatives, these are as follows:

1. Goods vehicles not exceeding 3.5 tonnes permissible maximum weight – *no records.*
2. Goods vehicles over 3.5 tonnes permissible maximum weight (including the weight of any trailer drawn) operating within EU rules – *tachograph records.*
3. Goods vehicles over 3.5 tonnes permissible maximum weight exempt from EU rules – *written 'logbook' records* (but subject to further exemption in certain cases).
4. Goods vehicles over 3.5 tonnes permissible maximum weight exempt from both EU and British domestic rules (eg military vehicles) – *no records.*

This chapter describes the record-keeping requirements applying to drivers falling within item 3 above, namely, those operating under the British domestic rules who must keep written 'logbook' records.

EXEMPTIONS FROM RECORD KEEPING

Written records do not have to be kept in the following cases:

- By drivers of vehicles which are exempt from 'O' licensing except that the exemption does not apply to drivers of Crown vehicles which would have needed an 'O' licence if the vehicle had not been Crown property.
- By drivers of goods vehicles on any day when they drive for four hours or less and within 50 kilometres of the vehicle's base (NB: this exemption is applicable only in the case of domestic operations – it does not apply to tachograph use – see page 65).
- By drivers voluntarily using an EU tachograph for record-keeping purposes which has been calibrated and sealed at a DETR-approved tachograph centre.

THE RECORD-KEEPING SYSTEM

From 29 September 1986 when the EU rules and British domestic hours rules last changed, a new style of simplified British record was introduced which relates specifically to the British domestic drivers' hours rules. Regulations brought the 'simplified' record book into use from 2 November 1987, with the old-type diagrammatic control book ceasing to have any further legal standing from that date.

RECORD BOOKS

Ready-printed record books can be purchased 'off the shelf' or firms can have their own version pre-printed with their own name and logo on the cover and individual weekly sheets if desired. In the latter case it is important that the specific requirements of the regulations are observed in both the format and the printing of the book.

The book must be a standard A6 format (105 mm × 148 mm) or larger if preferred. It must comprise:

- a front sheet on which is entered relevant information;
- a set of instructions for the use of the book;
- a number of individual weekly record sheets with facilities for completing these in duplicate (ie with carbon paper or carbonless copy paper); and
- a duplicate sheet which can be detached for return to the employer when completed.

There is no legal requirement for the numbering of record books or for their issue against an entry in a register of record book issues as previously required.

Weekly record sheets in the book must follow the format set out in the regulations with appropriate spaces for entries to be made under the following headings (see Figure 5.1):

- Driver's name.
- Period covered by sheet week commencing... week ending...

WEEKLY RECORD SHEETS

WEEKLY SHEETS							
1. DRIVER'S NAME			2. PERIOD COVERED BY SHEET WEEK COMMENCING (DATE) .... TO WEEK ENDING (DATE)................				
DAY ON WHICH DUTY COMMENCED	REGISTRATION NO. OF VEHICLE(S) 3.	PLACE WHERE VEHICLE(S) BASED 4.	TIME OF GOING ON DUTY 5.	TIME OF GOING OFF DUTY 6.	TIME SPENT DRIVING 7.	TIME SPENT ON DUTY 8.	SIGNATURE OF DRIVER 9.
MONDAY							
TUESDAY							
WEDNESDAY							
THURSDAY							
FRIDAY							
SATURDAY							
SUNDAY							
10. CERTIFICATION BY EMPLOYER			I HAVE EXAMINED THE ENTRIES IN THIS SHEET SIGNATURE .... POSITION HELD				

Figure 5.1 Simplified record sheet for British domestic transport operations

- Registration number of vehicle(s).
- Place where vehicle(s) based.
- Time of going on duty.
- Time of going off duty.
- Time spent driving.
- Time spent on duty.
- Signature of driver.
- Certification by employer (ie signature and position held).

ISSUE AND RETURN OF RECORD BOOKS

Employers must issue their employee drivers with record books when they are required to drive vehicles to which the British domestic drivers' hours regulations apply and where records must be kept.

Before issuing the book, the employer must complete the front cover to show the firm's name, address and telephone number, preferably with a rubber stamp if one is available.

When a record book is issued to the driver he or she should complete the front cover with:

- his or her surname;
- first name(s);
- date of birth;
- home address; and
- the date he or she first used the book.

When the book is completed the driver should also enter the date of the last entry (ie date of last use). The book also has space to record the name and address of a second employer.

Books issued by an employer to an employee-driver must be returned to that employer:

- when complete (subject to the requirement for the driver to retain it for two weeks after use); or
- when the employee leaves that employment.

Drivers must not take with them a record book issued by one employer when they join a new employer. When returning a record book to their employer under these circumstances, any unused weekly sheets and all duplicates must be included (ie left *in situ*).

Two employers or change of employer

Where a driver has two employers who employ him or her to drive goods vehicles to which the British domestic hours rules apply, the first employer must issue the record book as described above and completed weekly record sheets and completed record books must be returned to this employer.

The second employer must write or stamp his or her firm's name and address on the front cover of the record book with a statement that the holder is also a driver in his or her employment.

When a driver does part-time driving work for another employer he or she must disclose to each employer, if requested, details of his or her working and driving times with the other employer. Similarly, when a driver changes to a new employer the former employer must give the new employer details of the driver's previous driving and working times if requested.

RECORD BOOK ENTRIES

The driver must make entries on the weekly sheet for each day on which a record is required (instructions on the correct use of the book are printed inside the cover).

The driver must take care to ensure that an exact duplicate of the entry is made simultaneously (ie two separately written repeat entries are *not* acceptable even if no carbon paper is available). When completing a daily sheet the driver must enter all the required details under each of the headings. If the driver changes vehicles during the day, he or she must enter the registration number for each vehicle, and must then sign the sheet before returning it to his or her employer.

Completion of the record is straightforward, the driver having to enter only:

- the vehicle registration number (and the number for any subsequent vehicle driven);
- the time of coming on duty;

- the time at which he or she went off duty at the end of the day; and
- his or her signature.

The driver may enter any remarks concerning his or her entries, or point out corrections which should be made, in the appropriate box at the foot of the record sheet.

The employer may also use this space, if required, for making comments regarding the record. This space may also be used for recording the name of a second driver who accompanies the vehicle.

Corrections

Entries in the record book must be in ink or made by a ballpoint pen and there must be no erasures, corrections or additions. Mistakes may only be corrected by writing an explanation or by showing the correct information in the remarks space. Weekly sheets must not be mutilated or destroyed.

RETURN AND SIGNING OF RECORD SHEETS

When he or she has completed the weekly sheet and signed it, the driver must detach the duplicate copy from the book and hand it to his or her employer within seven days of the date of the last entry on the sheet. Within a further seven days the employer must examine and sign the duplicate sheet. However, if in either case it is not reasonably practicable to do so within this time, these actions must be carried out as soon as it is possible to do so.

RETENTION AND PRODUCTION OF RECORD BOOKS

Drivers should carry their record book with them at all times when working and must produce it for inspection at the request of an authorized examiner. The book should be shown to the employer at the end of every week or as soon as possible after the week, so that the employer can examine and countersign the entries.

Following completion of the book, drivers must continue to keep it with them for a further two weeks so as to have it available for inspection by the enforcement authorities if required. After this time, drivers should return the book to their employer.

Completed record books must be retained by the employer, also available for inspection by the enforcement authorities if required, for not less than 12 months (counting from the date of the last entry).

RECORD BOOKS FOR GERMANY

The German authorities require foreign drivers of light goods vehicles of between 2.8 tonnes and 3.5 tonnes gross weight (ie which are exempt from record keeping by means of the tachograph) entering the country to carry and complete AETR-type logbooks. These are the old-type logbooks long since abolished in the UK and the rest of Europe. Failure to carry such a logbook could result in delays and penalties.

CHECKING OF RECORDS

Police and examiners of the Vehicle Inspectorate (VI) can demand to see a driver's domestic record book, which he or she should carry at all times when on duty under the regulations.

A police officer (but not a VI examiner) may seize a record book if he or she considers it to be evidence of an offence.

6

WORKING TIME

INTRODUCTION

For many years, the transport industry alone had to contend with strict regulation of the working hours of its driver employees, with both British and EU law controlling the number of hours they could legally spend behind the wheel, their overall working time and the minimum breaks and rest periods they must take.

Now strict rules are applied to other employees under European Council Directive 93/104/EC of November 1993 (commonly referred to as the 'Working Time Directive' – WTD) which introduced a number of provisions to control working time for almost all employees. In particular, the Directive specified a maximum 48-hour working week and shift working restrictions under which night workers are not permitted to work more than an average of 8 hours in any 24-hour period. These requirements are enforced in the UK by our own domestic working time regulations (see below).

However, while this directive, which took effect in Great Britain from 1 October 1998, originally excluded the transport sector, a further directive known as the 'Horizontal

Amending Directive' (HAD) (Directive 2000/34/EC) came into force from 1 August 2003 amending the original WTD by setting rules for those employment sectors that were expressly excluded from the WTD, such as non-mobile transport workers and mobile workers not covered by the EU drivers' hours rules (for example, light vehicle drivers).

These EU directives are given the force of law in Great Britain by a number of regulations as follows:

- the Working Time Regulations 1998 (SI 1998 No. 1833);
- the Working Time Regulations 1999 (SI 1999 No. 3372) (amending regulations);
- the Working Time (Amendment) Regulations 2001 (SI 2001 No. 3256) (dealing mainly with annual leave);
- the Working Time (Amendment) Regulations 2002 (SI 2002 No. 3128) (dealing mainly with provisions regarding young people at work);
- the Working Time (Amendment) Regulations 2003 (SI 2003 No. 1684) (implementing the provisions of the HAD).

Finally, we have the Road Transport Directive (RTD) (Directive 2002/15/EC), which deals specifically with working time for those persons performing mobile transport activities within the scope of the EU drivers' hours rules (eg mainly LGV drivers). This directive is due to be implemented in the UK on 23 March 2005, subject to publication of the relevant Statutory Instrument. At present it is the subject of a UK public consultation document, the key proposals of which are outlined on pages 84–86. The consultation document can be viewed on the

DfT Web site at: www.dft.gov.uk (Freight Logistics, Consultation papers).

It is important to note that the RTD supplements both the current EU Drivers' Hours Regulation 3820/85/EEC and the AETR Agreement, so drivers who fall within the scope of these regulations when driving a goods vehicle must also take note of and comply with the provisions of the RTD.

LIMITATION ON WORKING TIME

The Working Time Regulations 1998 (as amended by 1999 regulations of the same name) came into force on 1 October 1998, implementing the EU Directive provisions in Great Britain only (ie Northern Ireland is excluded). The rules apply to most workers apart from those employed in:

- road, rail, sea and air transport;
- inland waterway and lake transport;
- sea fishing and other work at sea; and
- doctors in training.

Duty of employers

The regulations specifically require employers to ensure that working practices are adjusted to comply with the requirements of the directive on:

- average weekly working time;
- maximum night-time working and free health assessments;
- minimum daily rest periods;
- weekly rest periods;
- annual leave.

Weekly working

Average weekly working time must be limited to a maximum of 48 hours, including overtime, calculated over successive periods of 17 weeks (ie 4 months), or for the period of employment where this is less than 17 weeks.

Workers are permitted to agree with their employer, either individually or by means of a collective or workforce agreement, that the 48-hour maximum should not apply to them, but detailed working records of actual working hours must be kept.

NB: This opt-out facility is not to be extended to road haulage workers when they are eventually brought within the scope of the rules (see above and below).

Night working

Night working must be limited to a maximum of no more than 8 hours in 24 hours taken as an average over a 17-week reference period. However, night workers whose work involves special hazards or heavy physical or mental strain are limited to a maximum of a straight 8 hours in 24 hours with no averaging-out.

Employers must provide night workers with free health assessments and the opportunity to transfer to day work if their health is affected by night working.

NB: For these purposes, night workers are defined as being those who normally work, as part of their daily work, for at least three hours during night time. Night time is a period of at least seven hours, including the period between midnight and 5 am.

Daily rest

Employers must allow workers a daily rest period of at least 11 consecutive hours in each

24-hour period and an uninterrupted rest break of at least 20 minutes (away from their workstation if they have one) when their daily work exceeds six hours.

Weekly rest

Workers must be allowed a weekly rest period of not less than 24 hours in each seven days.

Young workers

Special restrictions apply to young workers (ie between 15 and 18 years) in regard to working between the hours of 10 pm and 6 am (the so-called 'restricted period'). In particular, they must have been offered a free health assessment both before being assigned to the work and at regular intervals subsequently.

Young workers must be allowed a 30-minute break after 4½ hours' work, taken away from their workstation if they have one.

Annual leave

Workers who have been employed continuously for 13 weeks are entitled to at least 4 weeks' paid annual leave which may not be exchanged for payment in lieu, except where it occurs on termination of the employment.

Record keeping

Employers must keep records of workers' hours of work which are adequate to show that the legal requirements have been complied with, and must retain them for at least two years from the date on which they were made.

Enforcement and penalties

These regulations impose a range of legal obligations on employers (as described above), enforceable by both the Health and Safety

Executive (HSE) and by local authorities in respect of premises for which they are responsible.

Failure by an employer to comply with any of the statutory provisions in this legislation is an offence under the Health and Safety at Work Act which may result in a fine of up to £5,000 on summary conviction and the risk of imprisonment on indictment by the Crown Court for more serious offences.

Unfair dismissal

The Employment Rights Act 1996 is amended by the addition of provisions to make it unfair to dismiss an employee for refusing to comply with a requirement contrary to the working time regulations, or to forgo their rights specified in the regulations.

THE ROAD TRANSPORT DIRECTIVE

This directive, which is due to be implemented in the UK from 23 March 2005, applies to mobile transport workers who are subject to the EU drivers' hours law (ie Regulation 3820/85/EEC), but excluding self-employed mobile workers who are to be exempt until 23 March 2009 (with a review of the situation two years before this date).

It is useful to consider the definition of certain terms used in the directive as follows:

- *Mobile transport activities* are any activity carried out by workers in the course of their employment within a road transport operation.
- A *mobile worker* is defined as any worker who forms part of the travelling staff of an undertaking that operates goods or

passenger transport for hire or reward or on its own account – obviously meaning drivers, but this also includes other crew members, trainees and apprentices.

- *Self-employed drivers* are similarly categorized (ie driving in a road transport operation) except that such workers are not tied to an employer by an employment contract.

- *Working time* is time spent at work and at the employer's disposal carrying out the employer's activities or duties. This includes such activities as working lunches, travelling as part of the job and work-related training, but not commuting between home and work, or rest breaks where no work is done or 'on-call' time when at home.

- *Periods of availability* are not working time and do not count as such, nor are they breaks or daily or weekly rest periods. They could include waiting time (for example, to load/unload or while waiting for a ferry) if the driver is free to dispose of his or her time during that period of waiting, but not if the driver had to remain with his or her vehicle in a queue – this would be working time. The key to this is whether the waiting period could have been foreseen in advance. If it could, it counts as non-working time; if it could not have been foreseen, it is working time. This will be fully defined in the forthcoming regulations and supporting guidance notes from the DfT.

- The *working week* is 48 hours' work averaged over a 4-month (ie 17-week) reference period – which may be extended to 6 months.

- *Breaks* during the working period must amount to a minimum of 30 minutes if working between 6 and 9 hours; or 45 minutes if working over 9 hours.
- *Night work* is to be defined as a 4-hour period between midnight and 4 am. Night working will be limited to 10 hours in any 24-hour period although a derogation will allow this to be extended.
- *Holidays* will comprise a minimum of 4 weeks (ie 20 days) paid at the average rate of earnings for the previous 12 weeks.

It is to be an important provision of the new regulations that mobile workers must tell their employer, in writing, of any hours they work for any other employer in any other job (even if it does not come within the scope of the RTD). Any such time worked will count towards the weekly WTD limit of 48 hours.

Record keeping
Irrespective of which directive applies (ie the WTD, HAD or RTD), employers must keep records of employee working time and provide copies of such records to their employees when asked to do so. There is no officially prescribed system for record keeping or special format for individual records, but whatever system is used the records must be kept for two years.

Health assessments
Employers are required to provide free health assessments for night workers. They have a duty to determine exactly who is a night worker for this purpose and provide the health assessment accordingly. The assessment should include a questionnaire devised and monitored by a

qualified health professional and, where necessary, backed up by a medical examination.

Enforcement

The regulations will be enforced by both the HSE and VOSA, the latter most likely in regard to workers covered by the RTD when they are checking compliance with the EU drivers' hours and tachograph rules.

Self-employed workers

As already mentioned, self-employed workers are to be exempted from inclusion in the WTD until 23 March 2009. But to qualify they must be genuinely self-employed in accordance with both RTD and Inland Revenue rules on self-employment. Basically, this means:

- not being tied to an employer under an employment contract;
- having freedom to organize their own work;
- their income must derive from the profits of their business; and
- they must have the freedom, either alone or in cooperation with others, to work for more than one customer.

EFFECTS OF THE LEGISLATION

Industry sources have predicted that application of these rules to road haulage will have significant implications both for current working practices and for costs. It is estimated that they are likely to result in the need for 80,000 additional drivers, costing overall some £5 billion annually.

Also, fears are being expressed that with the preferential treatment being meted out to self-employed drivers (ie the proposed three-year deferment), many haulage firms will seek to switch their employed drivers to self-employed status. Such an expansion of self-employment among drivers would mean many more workers engaging in non-recorded activities such as administration, dealing with accounts and VAT etc, and servicing, repairing and washing vehicles at weekends. This is seen as counterproductive in general health and safety terms and likely to lead directly to increased road safety risks.

7

DRIVERS' PAY AND EXPENSES

INTRODUCTION

The road haulage industry is notoriously flexible in its payment systems for drivers and other employees. Market forces dictate wage rates and conditions, more particularly so in the current climate of severe shortage in the experienced LGV driver pool. Surveys across the industry reveal wide variations between a low of around £5 or £5.50 per hour to £8 or £9 per hour. The TGWU is aiming to get all drivers on at least £10 per hour. A recent agreement in the West Midlands gives drivers £7.75 per hour for all hours worked. In this instance night work is paid at £7.45 per hour.

WAGE AGREEMENTS

Wages councils, of which at one time there were many, are now only few in number.

However, a few Joint Industrial Councils remain in being to negotiate wages in the hire and reward sector of road transport. They comprise road haulage employers and employees supported respectively by the Road Haulage Association (which provides a secretariat facility) and the trades unions.

The pay rates for drivers and other road haulage workers determined by the Councils are intended as benchmarks only and are not binding on the industry as a whole. Regional variations apply both in the categories of vehicles under which rates are classified and how the pay rates are stated – in some cases hourly rates, and in others weekly rates. Typical rates in 2004 for drivers of maximum weight vehicles are approximately £310 per 40-hour week to £380 plus for an over-50-hour week or regular night work.

THE NATIONAL MINIMUM WAGE

Besides any wage agreement that road haulage employers may have with their employees, they should be aware of the requirements of the national minimum wage provisions. These were introduced by the National Minimum Wage Regulations 1999 under the National Minimum Wage Act 1998 which came into force in the UK from 1 April 1999 and have been further amended by various National Minimum Wage (Amendment) Regulations.

These regulations require that workers (other than self-employed persons) aged 22 years or over must be paid at least £4.50 per hour, and workers aged from 18 to 21 years at least £3.80 per hour. The minimum wage applies to most workers in the UK, including agency workers (eg agency drivers), part-time and casual workers and those paid on a commission basis.

New workers aged 22 years or over who receive accredited training must be paid at least £3.80 per hour (the development rate) for the first six months. In this case, the employer will have to come to an agreement with the worker committing the employer to providing training on at least 26 days during that six-month period.

NB: *The above rates of pay are valid until 30 September 2004. From 1 October 2004 the rates will increase to £4.85, £4.10 and £4.10 per hour respectively.*

Assessing minimum pay

For the purposes of assessing minimum pay, payments to employees comprising bonuses, incentives, and performance-related awards count as part of the pay package, but other allowances not consolidated into an employee's pay are not counted. Similarly, overtime payments and shift payments do not count. Benefits in kind, such as the provision of overnight subsistence, meals, uniforms and work wear allowances, are also excluded.

Gross pay, with all deductions and reductions subtracted, should be divided by the number of hours worked to determine whether the resulting hourly pay rate at least matches, if not exceeds, the national minima stated above.

Types of work

The work hours that an employer has to pay for are calculated according the type of work on which employees are engaged. Mainly these are as follows:

- *Time work* is where an employee is paid for working a set number of hours or a set period of time.
- *Salaried work* is where an employee has a contract to work a set number of basic hours annually in return for an annual salary paid in equal instalments.

- *Unmeasured work* is where an employee is paid to do specific tasks (eg driving), but is not set specific hours for the work.

NB: In this case the employer must agree with the employee (in writing) a daily average of hours to be spent carrying out the assigned tasks. The employer must be able to show that the number of hours agreed is realistic.

Enforcement and penalties

Enforcement of the minimum wage provisions is by the Inland Revenue and by the employees themselves who have a right to complain if they are not being paid the national minimum wage.

Employers obviously need to keep accurate records of the hours worked and hourly rates paid to employees in case such information is called into question later – for a minimum of three years. An employee (or any other qualifying worker) may make a written request for access to his or her own records, and this must be allowed within 14 days unless extended by agreement. Should a dispute arise, the burden of proof is on the employer to show that the national minimum wage has been paid, not on the employee to prove that it has not.

Refusal to pay the national minimum wage is a criminal offence carrying a maximum fine up to £5,000 on conviction. Dismissal of an employee who becomes eligible for the national minimum wage or for a higher rate of pay will constitute unfair dismissal, with no qualifying period to be served by workers to secure protection against this form of unfair dismissal.

DRIVER OVERNIGHT ALLOWANCES

The amount paid to drivers for overnight subsistence varies considerably from area to area – the national general figure is currently £26.00 (2004 figure) applicable for nights out where no receipt is provided. Where alternative figures have been agreed, an annual increase of 9.3 per cent on the previously agreed figure is acceptable.

Tax relief on subsistence

The Inland Revenue has agreed that LGV drivers may be paid night-out allowances on a tax-free basis, where sleeper cabs are used, amounting to 75 per cent of the national figure which amounts to £19.50. This applies even if a locally agreed allowance is less than the national average. Where there are existing agreements with local tax offices for higher levels of subsistence payment, the tax-free allowance will be 75 per cent of the higher figure.

These payments should only be made where the employee does actually spend the night away and incurs extra expense. If the employee uses the bunk in a sleeper cab the allowable amount is only that required to meet the expenses he or she incurs, not the full night-out allowance.

Condition of payments

Payment of the above amounts is subject to the employer being satisfied that:

- the individual did necessarily spend the night away from home and normal place of work and that he or she used a sleeper cab;
- the employee necessarily incurred extra expense in doing so; and

- amounts paid are no more than reasonable reimbursement of the average allowable expenses of the driver (eg for payment of an evening meal, breakfast, washing facilities and the upkeep of bedding).

Owner drivers are dealt with differently for tax purposes and may NOT claim such night-out allowances against their tax liability.

Refusal of night-out claims

The Inland Revenue may refuse claims for tax-free payments of night-out allowances above the general limit. They may also query payment of night-out allowances where drivers have stayed only a few miles from base.

Payment above the national rate

Employers who pay in excess of the nationally agreed rate (or a locally agreed rate) without deduction of tax may find themselves liable to meet the tax due on the additional amounts paid, except where it can be proved that the expense was genuinely incurred (by production of a valid receipt). Alternatively, they should include the payment as part of the driver's wages within PAYE.

Charts retained for tax purposes

Where tachograph charts are used to justify payment of night-out and other subsistence expenses to drivers, these become part of the tax record and as such must be retained for six years instead of the normal one-year requirement applying to the charts under Regulation 3821/85 (see page 76).

MEAL EXPENSES

Where drivers receive from their employers a contribution towards midday meal expenses either by the issue of meal vouchers or by means of a cash payment, these contributions may be treated as not taxable provided they:

- are of a reasonable amount only (ie not exceeding £2.00 per day); and
- are paid to long-distance drivers only whose duties oblige them to take meals away from home and their normal place of employment, but not to drivers who have fixed or local routes.

Any amount paid in excess of £2.00 per day must be subject to income tax deduction unless acceptable evidence of the expenditure is provided to the employer or where the Inland Revenue has given dispensation.

Personal incidental expenses

Employee drivers may be paid additional amounts by way of 'personal incidental expenses' in relation to genuine expenditure (eg such as newspapers, laundry and calls home) during a qualifying absence (ie working away from home) up to a tax-free limit, without any tax consequences for the employee – or NI for the employer up to the value of £5 per day if in the UK or £10 per day outside the UK.

Source: Road Haulage Association Web site: www.rha.net/public/adviceandinfo/subsistence. shtml

Evidence of expenditure

The amount of relief that may be allowed depends mainly on the bills and vouchers that can be supplied by a driver in support of his or her claims. Employees who consider that they may have a potential claim should ensure that bills, receipts, etc are available in support of any claim for relief for the current tax year and future years; but if exceptionally they are unable on any occasion to obtain bills or receipts, they must make a note at the time of the date, place and amount spent. (Where the employer makes a contribution in cash or otherwise towards the cost of meals, this must be specified and the amount received set off against the expense in arriving at the net amount for which relief is claimed.) An expenses deduction cannot be given in the absence of evidence of expenditure and tax districts will not accept estimated figures of outgoings.

TAX RELIEF FOR INTERNATIONAL DRIVERS

International LGV drivers who spend less than 91 days in the UK during a tax year (ie from 6 April to 5 April annually) can claim 'non-resident' status and qualify for their wages to be paid tax-free. Previously, the limit was less than 60 days but this was increased to 91 days by the March 1998 Budget.

SELF-EMPLOYMENT

The road haulage industry is renowned for the number of self-employed workers, especially owner-driver lorry operators. However, not all such so-called self-employed persons are genuinely self-employed in terms that meet the legal requirements of the Inland Revenue (IR) and the Department for Work and Pensions (DWP) in regard to payment of National Insurance contributions.

To satisfy both the IR and the DWP a self-employed person must meet a series of so-called 'tests' under which they:

- decide, broadly, how and when specified work is to be carried out, the actual hours they work and when they take breaks and holidays and are not subject to disciplinary provisions of the employer;
- provide their own tools and equipment and are free to send another person (or subcontractor) in their place to carry out work where necessary;
- have no entitlement to payment for public or annual holidays or sickness; are not included in the employer's pension scheme, and have no rights to claim redundancy payments, unfair dismissal or any entitlement to unemployment benefit if their services are no longer required;
- take financial risk with the aim of making a profit, are responsible for paying their own income tax and national insurance contributions, and charge for their services by submitting an invoice;
- are free to work for other employers as required if they so wish (a self-employed person who works for only one employer is likely to be considered to be an employee of that employer).

A number of instances have arisen in transport where the Inland Revenue has questioned the self-employed status of owner-drivers (mainly because they work for only one firm). In such cases, where the IR has ruled that owner-driver agreements are merely employment contracts, the employer becomes liable for back tax and NI contributions for its subcontractors. This is especially so where the owner-driver works under the 'O' licence of the employing company – and if he or she is genuinely self-employed then, in any event, this practice is illegal under 'O' licensing legislation.

Self-employment under the RTD

The Road Transport Directive (due to come into force from 23 March 2005) introduces a particular definition for self-employed workers who will be exempt from the directive until March 2009 as follows:

> self-employed driver shall mean anyone whose main occupation is to transport passengers or goods by road for hire or reward within the meaning of Community legislation under cover of a Community licence or any other professional authorisation to carry out the aforementioned transport, who is entitled to work for himself and who is not tied to an employer by an employment contract or by any other type of working hierarchical relationship, who is free to organize the relevant working activities, whose income depends directly on the profits made and who has the freedom to, individually or through a co-operation between self-employed drivers, have commercial relations with several customers.

NB: *It should be noted that the above definition under the RTD is not the same as the definition under the Employment Rights Act 1996, or under the Working Time Regulations 1998, nor is the test for self-employment the same as that applied by the Inland Revenue – see page 97.*

8

DRUGS, TIREDNESS AND STRESS

INTRODUCTION

Drivers' health and their ability to work efficiently and drive safely can be significantly affected by their work. Three aspects are of particular concern:

- the effects of using illegal drugs and certain prescribed medicines;
- tiredness; and
- work-related stress.

These all contribute in some measure to the creation of greater safety risks on the road (and are actually proven to be a primary cause in some fatal and serious injury accidents) and in other areas of the driver's work such as loading and unloading etc. For this reason it was thought useful to include some helpful advice here on these matters.

DRUGS AND DRIVING

According to official sources, drugs are a major cause of one in five fatal road accidents. Another source says that driving after smoking cannabis could be a greater danger than drink-driving, and that as many as three million people could be driving under the influence of this drug. Yet another report has highlighted the fact that drivers who use tranquillizers are involved in 1,600 road accidents every year – 110 of them fatal.

Many reasons may explain why an individual turns to drugs. Peer group, social and lifestyle pressure may be a major influence, but there is no doubt that pressure at work and the strain of long-distance driving and having to meet tight delivery schedules are important contributory factors in the case of transport industry workers. Whatever the cause, the resultant consequences can be very grave with, as we have seen above, the risk of a fatal road accident as the ultimate penalty.

Illegal drugs

Among the illegal drugs which may be detected and which can adversely affect driving are:

- cannabis, which produces slow reaction times (may remain detectable in the blood for up to 90 days);
- cocaine, which may increase reaction times, but severely affects accuracy and judgement, and also has the potential to cause hallucination;
- amphetamines, which may increase reaction times in the short term, but severely affects accuracy and judgement;
- ecstasy, which may increase reaction times, but severely affects accuracy and judgement;
- heroin, which produces reduced reaction times and causes drowsiness and sleep.

Prescribed drugs

Prescribed tranquillizers, sedatives and anti-depressants, as well as diabetes and epilepsy drugs, albeit legal in that they are authorized for use of the person by his or her doctor, may nevertheless have an adverse effect on a driver's judgement and reactions and therefore increase the risk of an accident.

These include a number of anti-anxiolytic benzodiazepines (prescribed to reduce stress and anxiety), including:

- Valium;
- Librium;
- Ativan.

The sedative effect of these drugs is substantially compounded by the addition of alcohol, even when taken in relatively small quantities, resulting in a potentially significant loss of coordination. Similarly, sleeping tablets (eg diazepam, temazepam and nitrazepam), including the new drug zopiclone, may also have a continuing sedative effect on a driver the following morning. Furthermore, a whole range of other proprietary medicines such as strong painkillers, antihistamines, cold and flu remedies, eye drops, cough medicines and other common painkillers taken in sufficient quantities may have similar effects.

Warning signs of drug abuse include:

- hangover;
- repeated late arrival for work;
- mood changes;
- an inability to concentrate;
- irritability and aggression with work mates;
- impaired job performance;

- an obvious shortage of money (eg typified by borrowing etc);
- a tendency to criminal activities such as theft to pay for drugs.

Generally, individuals suffering the effects of drug abuse fail to recognize any or all of the above symptoms in themselves – and this too is a further indicator of the situation and why such people are a great danger to themselves and to others.

In the case of truck drivers, if they feel drowsy, dizzy, confused, or suffer other side effects that could affect their reaction times or judgement, they should not drive, or if already on a journey, they should stop and rest and/or seek help. Continuing to drive could lead to an accident in which they and other innocent people could be injured or even killed.

Drug testing

The police carried out drug testing trials on drivers during random roadside spot checks in Spring 1998. Principally the scheme was designed to test the 'Drugwipe' testing kit that is wiped across the driver's forehead to pick up any traces of drugs in his or her sweat. This is a foretaste of what may become standard practice.

Drug testing of LGV drivers by their employers is becoming an increasing practice in the UK, especially among tanker fleet operators, following the pattern in the USA which has had mandatory testing since 1992. In fact, Unilabs UK, one of the leading drug testing laboratories, has reported a substantial increase in requests for testing by haulage companies in recent times. While there is no suggestion at this stage that the practice should become mandatory in this country, most of Britain's major oil companies now carry out random testing for both alcohol and drug problems – Shell has produced a staff booklet identifying 11 banned substances (including amphetamines) and warning of the consequences of drink or drug abuse.

In mid-2000, emergency tests were introduced for all road users because of a sharp rise in drug-related road deaths. Drivers suspected of having taken drugs are being asked to walk a straight line and count their steps, among other physical tests. Suspects are taken to a police station for further tests. Fines of up to £5,000 may be imposed on convicted offenders, together with a mandatory driving ban and risk of a prison sentence.

Useful guidance on this matter is contained in Unilabs' brochure *Drug Abuse – The Facts* obtainable from the company at: Bewlay House, 32 Jamestown Road, London NW1 7BY (tel: 020 7267 2672; fax: 020 7267 2551).

JOIN THE FIGHT AGAINST DRUGS

If you have any information about drugs or drug smugglers, HM Customs request that you ring their 24-hour hotline 0800 59 5000. You don't have to tell Customs who you are, and for important information you may be eligible for a cash reward.

Tiredness can kill

DfT-sponsored studies have shown that tiredness can kill, hence its campaign of this name to combat tiredness amongst both car and LGV drivers.

Tiredness at the wheel has been established as the principal factor in around 10 per cent of all road accidents and in 20 per cent of motorway accidents, and is thought to account for up to 300 road deaths a year. Most accidents of this type involve men and at least half of all the drivers involved are under 30 years of age.

The main points for drivers to observe are that they should:

- make sure they are fit to drive, particularly before undertaking any long journeys (over an hour) – avoid such journeys in the morning without a good night's sleep or in the evening after a full day's work;
- avoid undertaking long journeys between midnight and 6am, when natural alertness is at a minimum;
- plan their journey to take sufficient breaks – a minimum break of at least 15 minutes after every two hours' driving is advised;
- if they feel at all sleepy, stop in a safe place and either take a nap for around 15 minutes, or drink two cups of strong coffee.

WORK-RELATED STRESS

It is well known that working situations can cause stress, which may manifest itself in the health of employees and consequently in the risk of accidents in the workplace. In fact, work-related stress is becoming recognized as a major cause of employee illness and absenteeism.

All employers have a duty in law to ensure that their employees are not made ill by their work. Transport employers particularly need to recognize that the stress created in driving situations can make their employees ill.

Stress is a person's natural reaction to excessive pressure – it is not a disease. However, excessive and long-term stress can lead to mental and physical ill health, causing, for example, depression, nervous breakdown and even heart disease. Stress in one person can lead to stress in other people who have to cover their work.

The costs of stress can be high for the employer by way of:

- high staff turnover;
- increased absence through sickness;
- reduced work performance;
- increased lateness;
- more customer complaints; and
- greater risk of accidents at work.

An employer who ignores signs of stress among employees or who fails to take the necessary action to reduce stress may face claims for compensation from employees who have suffered ill health from work-related stress.

Where stress has been caused in a workplace, or made worse by work, it is the employer's duty to assess the risks among employees, in particular:

- looking for pressures at work that could cause high and long-lasting levels of stress;
- deciding which employees may be affected or harmed by the stress;
- deciding whether sufficient measures are being taken to prevent harm from stress;
- determining what further measures can be taken to reduce the stress-inducing pressures of work.

Employers are not responsible for preventing ill health from stress caused by problems occurring outside work, but they should be able to recognize the effects of such stress – for example, people being unable to cope with their work, or performing below their normal standard. In such cases, adopting an understanding attitude would be helpful to the individual concerned and in the employer's best interests.

9

NEW-GENERATION DIGITAL TACHOGRAPHS

INTRODUCTION

A new generation of digital tachographs will be fitted to newly registered vehicles from 2005 and will run alongside existing analogue instruments for the foreseeable future, probably causing a great deal of confusion, to say nothing of the cost to the industry of retraining existing drivers on another system and newcomers on both systems.

EU Regulation 1360/02/EC amends the current tachograph regulation 3821/85/EC accordingly.

This regulation became law throughout all member states of the European Union 24 months after publication of the regulation and its new technical annex (Annex 1B) in the *Official Journal of the European Communities* (the OJ) on 5 August 2002. Newly registered vehicles have to be fitted with the new-type digital instruments in which the driver inserts his or her own, personalized, micro-chip 'smart' card on which his or her driving, working and rest activities are held, along with vehicle speeds and distances driven, for up to 28 days.

There are no plans for retrospective fitment of digital tachographs to existing vehicles except that where, after the official date mentioned above, a pre-existing vehicle suffers tachograph failure requiring replacement of the instrument, the replacement will have to be of the new type.

NEW LEGAL PROVISIONS

As stated above, the long-awaited digital – 'smart' card – tachograph regulation 1360/2002/EC – amending regulation 3821/85/EEC – and its technical Annex 1B were published in the *Official Journal of the European Communities* on 5 August 2002. This date signalled the start of an official 24-month countdown to the date when such instruments must be fitted and used in relevant vehicles.

Thus from 5 August 2004 (deferred to 5 August 2005 owing to technical difficulties with instrument testing and type approval), the following vehicles will be required to be fitted with digital tachographs:

- all new goods vehicles over 3.5 tonnes gross weight (apart from those specifically exempt under the legislation); and
- existing 'in-service' vehicles over 12 tonnes gross weight in which the existing analogue tachograph fails and has to be replaced.

Some vehicle manufacturers are expected to start installing these instruments in new vehicles prior to the 'due' date, and driver 'smart' cards are likely to be issued by the Driver and Vehicle Licensing Agency (DVLA) from 2004 to allow for driver training and familiarization.

NEW REGULATIONS

The existing Regulation 3821/85/EEC has been amended firstly by Regulation 2135/98/EC and then by Regulation 1360/2002/EC for a number of reasons, including:

- to prevent infringement and fraud in application of the drivers' hours rules;
- to monitor automatically driver performance and behaviour;
- to overcome problems of monitoring compliance due to the numbers of individual record sheets (charts) which have to be held in the vehicle cab;
- the need to introduce advance recording equipment with electronic storage devices and personal driver cards to provide an indisputable record of work done by the driver over the last few days and the vehicle over a period of several months; and
- to devise a system which ensures total security of the recorded data.

Definitions for digital tachographs and ancillaries

The new-type equipment will feature a number of key components defined in the regulations as follows:

- *Recording equipment* is amended to mean the total equipment intended for installation in road vehicles to show, record and store automatically or semi-automatically details of the movement of such vehicles and of certain work periods of their drivers. This equipment includes cables, sensors, an electronic driver information device, one (two) card reader(s) for the insertion of one or two driver memory card(s), an integrated or separate printer, display instruments, facilities for downloading the data memory, facilities to display or print information on demand and facilities for the input of the places where the daily work period begins and ends.

- *Data memory* means an electronic storage system built into the recording equipment, capable of storing at least 365 calendar days from the recording equipment. The memory should be protected in such a way as to prevent unauthorized access to and manipulation of the data and detect any such attempt.
- A *driver card with memory* means a removable information transfer and storage device allocated by the authorities of the Member States to each individual driver for the purposes of identification of the driver and storage of essential data. The format and technical specifications of the driver card must meet the requirements laid down in the technical annex to the regulations (not yet adopted).
- A *control card* means a removable data transfer and storage device for use in the card reader of the recording equipment, issued by the authorities of the Member States to competent authorities to get access to the data stored in the data memory or in the driver cards for reading, printing and/or downloading.
- A *company data card* means a removable data transfer and storage device issued by the Member State's authorities to the owner of vehicles fitted with recording equipment. The company data card allows for displaying, downloading and printing of the

data stored in the recording equipment fitted in the company's vehicle(s).

- *Downloading* means the copying of a part or of a complete set of data stored in the data memory of the vehicle or in the memory of the driver card, but which does not alter or delete any stored data, allows for the origin of downloaded data to be authenticable and to be kept in a format that can be used by any authorized person and ensures that any attempts to manipulate data are detectable.

Functions of digital instruments

The regulations require digital instruments to be able to record, store, display and print out specified statutory information as follows (see also Figure 9.1).

Figure 9.1 Illustration of new-type digital tachograph installation in vehicle, showing the speedometer and clock and the recording equipment

Recording and storing in the data memory

The instrument will be required to record and store:

- distance travelled by the vehicle with an accuracy of 1 km;
- speed of the vehicle:
  - momentary speed of the vehicle at a frequency of 1 s for the last 24 hours of use of the vehicle;
  - exceeding the authorized speed of the vehicle, defined as any period of more than 1 minute during which the vehicle speed exceeds 90 km/h for N3 vehicles or 105 km/h for M3 vehicles (with time, date, maximum speed of the over-speeding, average speed during the period concerned);
- periods of driving time (times and dates), with an accuracy of 1 minute;
- other periods of work or of availability (times and dates) with an accuracy of 1 minute;
- breaks from work and daily rest periods (times and dates) with an accuracy of 1 minute;
- for electronic recording equipment, which is equipment operated by signals transmitted electrically from the distance and speed sensor, any interruption exceeding 100 milliseconds in the power supply of the recording equipment (except lighting), in the power supply of the distance and speed sensor and any interruption in the signal lead to the distance and speed sensor, with date, time, duration and driver card issue number;
- the driver card issue number with times and dates of insertion and removal;

- for each driver card that is inserted for the first time after it was used in another item of recording equipment:
  - current driving time since the last break or rest period,
  - driving time for the day after the last rest period of at least eight hours,
  - driving times for the day between two rest periods of at least eight hours for the preceding 27 calendar days with date, time and duration,
  - total of the driving times for the current week and the preceding week and the total of the driving times of the two completed preceding weeks,
  - rest periods of at least eight hours' duration for the day and the preceding 27 calendar days in each case with date, time and duration,
  - the VRN (vehicle registration number) of the vehicles driven;
- date, time and duration of driving without an inserted or a functioning driver card;
- data recorded on the places at which the daily work period began and ended;
- automatically identifiable system faults of the recording equipment with date, time and driver card issue number;
- faults in the driver card with date and time and driver card issue number;
- workshop card number of the authorized fitter or workshop with the date of at least the last installation inspection and/or periodic inspection of the recording equipment;
- control card number with date of control card insertion and type of control (display, printing, downloading). In case of

downloading, period downloaded should be recorded;

- time adjustment with date, time and card issue number;
- driving status (single/crew driving – driver/co-driver).

Storing on the driver card

The driver card must be capable of storing:

- the essential data for a period of at least the last 28 calendar days combined with the VRN identification of the vehicle driven and the data as required above;
- the events and faults mentioned above with the VRN identification of the vehicle driven;
- the date and time of insertion and removal of the driver card and distance travelled during the corresponding period;
- the date and time of insertion and removal of the co-driver card with issue number.

Data must be recorded and stored on the driver card in such a way as to rule out any possibility of falsification.

Recording and storing for two drivers

Where vehicles are used by two drivers, the driving time must be recorded and stored on the driver card of the driver who is driving the vehicle. The equipment must record and store in the data memory and on the two driver cards simultaneously, but distinctly, details of the information listed above.

Displaying or printing for an authorized examiner

The equipment must be capable of displaying or printing, on request, the following information:

- driver card issue number, expiry date of the card;
- the surname and first name of the driver who is the cardholder;
- current driving time since the last break or rest period;
- driving time for the day after the last rest period of at least eight hours;
- driving times for the day between two rest periods of at least eight hours for the preceding 27 calendar days on which the driver has driven, with date, time and duration;
- total of the driving times for the current week and the preceding week and the total times for the two completed preceding weeks;
- the other periods of work and availability;
- rest periods of at least eight hours' duration for the day and the preceding 27 days in each case with date, time and duration;
- VRN identification of vehicles driven for at least the last 28 calendar days with the distance travelled per vehicle and day, time of first insertion and last removal of the driver card and the time of change of vehicle;
- time adjustment with date, time and card issue number;
- interruption of power supply to the recording equipment with date, time, duration and driver card issue number;
- sensor interruption with date, time, duration and driver card issue number;
- the VIN and/or VRN identification of the vehicle driven;
- driving without driver card as defined above for the last 28 calendar days;

- details of the information stored concerning the driver;
- recorded data on the places where the daily work period began and ended;
- the automatically identifiable system faults of the recording equipment with date, time and driver card issue number;
- the faults in the driver card with date and time and driver card issue number;
- control card number with date of control card insertion and type of control (display, printing, downloading). In the case of downloading, period downloaded should be recorded;
- exceeding the authorized speed as defined above, with date, time and driver card issue number for the current week and in any case including the last day of the previous week;
- summary reports to permit compliance with the relevant regulations to be checked.

Typical equipment

In advance of introduction of statutory requirements for the mandatory fitment of digital tachographs, the key tachograph manufacturers have shown prototype models built to the outline specification included in Regulations 2135/98/EC and 1360/2002/EC. Typical of such equipment is that made by VDO Kienzle (as shown in Figure 9.2), comprising a recording unit incorporating a mass memory fitted into the vehicle instrument panel. This is connected to an intelligent sensor to enable transmission of 'driving' pulses to the recording unit and to the instrument cluster for displaying road speed, time and distance travelled. Connections are provided (ie data interfaces) to allow readout of the stored data via an office

PC or a laptop computer, and for it to be printed out to hard copy via a suitable printer where required. Various warning functions are incorporated and a keypad connection can be made to input additional commands and relevant data.

Crucial to the whole system is the driver ('smart') card (a credit-card-sized plastic card with an embedded microchip) that is personal to the individual and carries identification information and other essential data about him or her. It has a capacity to store relevant data on driving and working times, breaks and rest periods etc covering at least 28 days and will comprise the legal record in place of the current tachograph chart. The card itself must be tamper-proof and strict regulatory systems are to be established by national governments to prevent fraudulent issue, use and transfer of cards within their territories.

Advice for drivers on use of the 'smart' card tachograph

The biggest difference for drivers between the current (analogue-type) tachograph and the new digital tachograph will be the use of a **'smart' card (officially called a 'tachograph card')** instead of the current type of chart (ie record sheet) used in analogue tachographs. This is a plastic card similar in size to a photo driving licence or credit card, with a microchip in it.

The driver card is just one of the set of four such cards used with digital tachographs, the others being:

- company cards – for use by vehicle operators to protect and download the data;
- workshop cards – available only to approved tachograph calibration centres;

- control cards – for use only by VOSA examiners and the police for carrying out enforcement activities.

Before **commencing a journey** the driver will be required to insert his or her driver card into the first (driver) or second (co-driver) person slot on the front of the Vehicle Unit (VU) in much the same way that a chart is put into the head of an analogue tachograph. The 'centre field' details, which the driver currently has to enter on the chart, with digital instruments, will be recorded automatically by the tachograph – ie driver name, vehicle registration number, start and finish odometer readings and name of place code.

In the same way that drivers and co-drivers currently **record their different activities** – driving, other work, breaks and rest – by changing the mode switch and by swapping the position of charts in the tachograph head, digital 'smart' cards will need to be swapped between driver and co-driver slots in the instrument when two drivers operate a vehicle.

Details of time spent **working away** from the vehicle that are currently written on the rear of the tachograph chart (ie record sheet) will have to be input manually into the digital tachograph. The system will also record details of any faults, interference, errors and over-speeding that occur.

All this information will be stored for at least **28 days** on the driver's personal 'smart' card and for at least a year in the Vehicle Unit.

NB: *Further information on digital tachographs can be found on the official government Web site: www.digitaltachograph.gov.uk.*

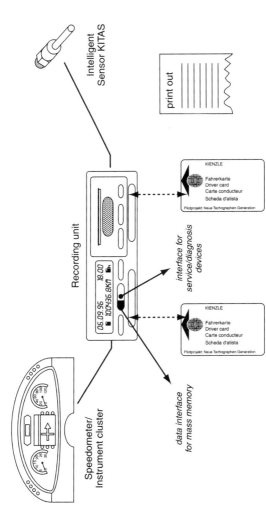

Figure 9.2 Layout of digital tachograph equipment in vehicle, showing representation of two driver cards (ie for double-manned vehicle operation)

Appendix

EXEMPTIONS TO EU HOURS AND TACHOGRAPH RULES

The EU regulations list a number of exemptions (derogations) that apply internationally and further exemptions which national governments are permitted to make if they so wish. These are shown below.

International exemptions

1. Vehicles not exceeding 3.5 tonnes gross weight, including the weight of any trailer drawn.
2. Passenger vehicles constructed to carry not more than nine persons including driver.
3. Passenger vehicles on regular services on routes not exceeding 50 kilometres.
4. Vehicles with legal maximum speed not exceeding 30 kph (approx 18.6 mph).
5. Vehicles used by armed services, civil defence, fire services, forces responsible for maintaining public order (ie police).
6. Vehicles used in connection with sewerage; flood protection; water, gas and electricity services; highway maintenance and control; refuse collection and disposal*; telephone and telegraph services; carriage of postal articles**; radio and television broadcasting; detection of radio or television transmitters or receivers.

*NB: It has been ruled that privatized firms operating refuse collection services on behalf of local authorities are exempt from the EU hours rules in the same way that local authority-owned refuse vehicle drivers were exempt prior to privatization of the service. A subsequent case made it clear that this exemption applies only where refuse collection operations are carried out over short distances – not long-haul waste operations.

**NB: The DTLR has ruled that this exemption from the EU drivers' hours rules applies equally to parcel carriers operating in competition with the Royal Mail (ie the Parcelforce service) as to the Royal Mail itself. Instead, these operations fall within the scope of the British domestic hours rules as described in this chapter. However, despite this exemption, the EU tachograph rules still apply to such operations.

7. Vehicles used in emergencies or rescue operations.
8. Specialized vehicles used for medical purposes.
9. Vehicles transporting circus and funfair equipment.
10. Specialized breakdown vehicles.
11. Vehicles undergoing road tests for technical development, repair or maintenance purposes, and new or rebuilt vehicles which have not yet been put into service.
12. Vehicles used for non-commercial carriage of goods for personal use (ie private use).
13. Vehicles used for milk collection from farms and the return to farms of milk containers or milk products intended for animal feed.

National exemptions (under British derogations)

1. Passenger vehicles constructed to carry not more than 17 persons including driver.
2. Vehicles used by public authorities to provide public services that are not in competition with professional road hauliers.
3. Vehicles used by agricultural, horticultural, forestry or fishery* undertakings, for carrying goods within a 50 km radius of the place where the vehicle is normally based, including local administrative areas, the centres of which are situated within that radius.

* NB: To gain this exemption the vehicle must be used to carry live fish or to carry a catch of fish which has not been subjected to any process or treatment (other than freezing) from the place of landing to a place where it is to be processed or treated.

4. Vehicles used for carrying animal waste or carcasses not intended for human consumption.
5. Vehicles used for carrying live animals from farms to local markets and vice versa, or from markets to local slaughterhouses.
6. Vehicles specially fitted for and used:
    – as shops at local markets and for door-to-door selling;
    – for mobile banking, exchange or savings transactions;
    – for worship;
    – for the lending of books, records or cassettes;
    – for cultural events or exhibitions.
7. Vehicles (not exceeding 7.5 tonnes pmw) carrying materials or equipment for the

driver's use in the course of his work within a 50km radius of base provided the driving does not constitute the driver's main activity and does not prejudice the objectives of the regulations.

8. Vehicles operating exclusively on islands not exceeding 2,300 km^2 not linked to the mainland by bridge, ford or tunnel for use by motor vehicles (this includes the Isles of Wight, Arran and Bute).

9. Vehicles (not exceeding 7.5 tonnes pmw) used for the carriage of goods propelled by gas produced on the vehicle or by electricity.

10. Vehicles used for driving instruction (but not if carrying goods for hire or reward).

11. Tractors used exclusively for agricultural and forestry work.

12. Vehicles used by the RNLI for hauling lifeboats.

13. Vehicles manufactured before 1 January 1947.

14. Steam-propelled vehicles.

15. Vintage vehicles (ie over 25 years old) not carrying more than nine persons including the driver, not being used for profit, and being driven to or from a vintage rally, museum, public display or a place where it has been or is to be repaired, maintained or tested.

16. Operations carried out in exceptional circumstances (subject to DETR approval and provided the safety objectives of the regulations are not jeopardized).

17. Tachographs are not required in vehicles used for the collection of sea coal.

Note: In exemption 2 above relating to vehicles used by public authorities, the exemption applies only if the vehicle is being used by:

(a) a health authority in England and Wales, a health board in Scotland or a National Health Service (NHS) Trust:
   – to provide ambulance services in pursuance of its duty under the NHS Act 1977 or NHS (Scotland) Act 1978; or
   – to carry staff, patients, medical supplies or equipment in pursuance of its general duties under the Act;

(b) a local authority to fulfil social services functions, such as services for old persons or for physically and mentally handicapped persons;

(c) HM Coastguard or lighthouse authorities;

(d) port authorities within port limits;

(e) airports authority within airport perimeters;

(f) British Rail successor publicly owned companies, London Regional Transport, a Passenger Transport Executive or local authority for maintaining railways;

(g) British Waterways Board for maintaining navigable waterways.

NB: Under a European Court ruling, British Gas must fit tachographs to vehicles it uses for the delivery of gas appliances, gas cylinders and meters to ensure fair competition with private transport operators. The point at issue, and contended by British Gas, was that its vehicles engaged on such deliveries were being used in connection with gas services.

NNB: Vehicles used for private waste collection (ie not on behalf of local authorities) on journeys exceeding 50 km radius from the place where they are normally based must be fitted with a fully calibrated tachograph, following a European Court of Justice ruling.

INDEX

Other books by the author:

A Study Manual of Professional Competence in Road Haulage, 11th edn, 2004

The Dictionary of Transport and Logistics: contains over 3,000 terms and abbreviations, 2002

The Professional LGV Driver's Handbook, 2nd edn, 2004

The Transport Manager's and Operator's Handbook 2004, 34th edn

The Certificate of Professional Competence: 1001 typical questions and answers, 4th edn, 2001

The Dangerous Goods Safety Manual: A study guide for DGSAs, 2000

Also available from Kogan Page:

The Handbook of Logistics and Distribution Management, 2nd edn, 2000, Alan Rushton, John Oxley and Phil Croucher

Managing Passenger Logistics, 2000, Paul Fawcett

International Transport, 5th edn, 1999, Rex Faulks

An Introduction to Transport Studies, 3rd edn, 1998, John Hibbs

Applied Transport Economics, 3rd edn, 2004, Stuart Cole

The Directory of UK Food Transport & Logistics 2004, 2003, Minto Gordon

Global Logistics and Distribution Planning, 4th edn, 2003, Donald Waters

Managing Transport Operations, 3rd edn, 2002, Edmund J Gubbins

Logistics and Retail Management, 2nd edn, 2004, edited by John Fernie and Leigh Sparks

Transport Economies and Policy: A practical analysis of performance efficiency and marketing objectives, 2003, John Hibbs

The above titles are available from all good bookshops or direct from the publishers. To obtain more information, please contact the publishers at the address below:

Kogan Page
120 Pentonville Road
London N1 9JN
Tel: 020 7278 0433
Fax: 020 7837 6348
www.kogan-page.co.uk